AF556093

Feminizing the Labour Relations

Transition in Production Roles of Female Labour from Farm to Non-Farm in a Telangana Village

Feminizing the Labour Relations

Transition in Production Roles of Female Labour from Farm to Non-farm in a Telangana Village

M. Vanamala

First Published, 2016

ISBN 978-93-83723-13-3

Published by
LG PUBLISHERS DISTRIBUTORS
49, Gali No. 14, Pratap Nagar
Mayur Vihar Phase I, Delhi 110 091
Tel : 011 2279 5641 email: lgpdist@gmail.com

Printed at
Saurabh Printer, Greater Noida

Contents

Foreword

TRANSITION WITH GENDERED PRECARIOUSNESS

Structural transformation and its impact on the lives and livelihoods of different communities, classes and sections of people forms the core concern of development studies. In a relatively long drawn process of development of societies, there are short periods marked by epochal changes. In the development history of post-Independent India, last three decades between 1980 and 2010 could be considered as a period that witnessed one such epochal change. There were as many shifts in production and employment structures as much as in the institutional and policy approaches. This was the period that saw definitive initiation and spread of the process of liberalization, privatization and globalization. From an economic regime the past where the state assumed commanding heights, the period witnessed the retreat of the state to the role of a facilitator, leaving the economy to be driven by market incentives that promote profits for growth. The shift was from growth with distributive justice to the primacy of growth per se that was assumed to trickle down to those at the bottom. It was also a period of accelerated growth, though not to the heights of 'India Shining' illusion that was sought to created, but certainly in contrast with the notoriously low 'Hindu rate of growth' of the earlier period. A comprehensive analysis of the changes in the economy and society during this period becomes imperative to understand the nature of development process and the condition of the 'doings and beings' of the people of India. And as could be expected, there have been a large number of well documented studies on the nature of structural transformation, the factors behind the growth process and its welfare implications. The nature of growth in the period and its unequalising impact are widely debated. And of course, in the name of development, there was an overdose of everything being seen from growth on poverty angle and in the process making people to suspect and question the very idea of development. Most of these studies and debates were largely confined to macro level changes. Even studies focused on social groups, workers or women are mostly at the macro level. There are hardly any systematic analyses of the kind of structural changes and their impact on the work opportunities and the nature of working and living conditions of different sections of people at the micro level. It is in this context, the present study, by Dr. Vanamala, focused on the impact of new industrialization process in a predominantly agriculture dependent village on women and work during critical period of transition of the last three decades (1979-2010), assumes a significant place in the development literature.

The basic question that is sought to be answered is as to what happens to women's work and status if a village in which they are mostly employed in agriculture, except for some traditional cottage crafts, undergoes a rapid transition to industrial and other modern non-farm activities? For this apparently simple question the answer lies in complex layers of analysis. The first step is to track changes in agriculture, beginning with land use, the changes in the share of area cultivated, the changes in the cropping pattern in the area that continues to be under cultivation, the nature of agricultural technology in terms of gender-specific labour use and the relative female wages. This part has been done with admirably painstaking fieldwork involving sample survey of agricultural households in three rounds beginning with 1979-80, a second round in 1995-96 and the final survey in 2009-10. The detailed household data are not only on work status, employment sources but also costs and returns in agriculture as much as changing asset position in non-agriculture. The primary data are placed in context by drawing on the secondary sources of information including consultations with official functionaries. The second step is to relate the basic changes in the village to the emerging larger policy and institutional changes at the national level. The larger macro context was the emergence of the neoliberal regime in which private profit seeking activities across all sectors, including health and education, had all the incentives, while state's role was gradually minimized even in agricultural support like extension and input subsidies. At the state level there were several critical institutional changes, of which one with far reaching consequence for the rural power structure was the abolition of the institution of "patwary", the hereditary village office, which was invariably the bastion of the dominant castes. This was followed by the amendment to the Panchayat Raj Act providing for reservations in the three-tier Panchayat Institutions as a result of the 73rd Amendment of the Constitution. These two institutional changes had far reaching changes in the social base of rural power structure. There were other changes like the decline of joint family system along with increasing partition of landed property and with it growing land related litigation, the weakening of caste-based community organizations, the acquisition of land for industrial and other purposes like real estate, increase in the land market operations and emergence of the nexus between revenue officials, the village *Sarpanch* and the real estate speculators and the resulting manipulations often resulting in strained relations between the nexus and the farming community, which was often reflected in discrimination in the distribution of welfare measures like providing ration cards, health cards, old age and disability pensions, and even in fixing property taxation for the residential houses. The MGNREGS added to the autonomy and bargaining power of the wage workers. These changes show that during the past three decades the village which was a community governed by a kind of semi-feudal authority flowing from the caste-land based hierarchy was transformed into a group of households each trying to find a place of its own in the fast emerging market economy.

It is in this broad narrative of changing economic and social institutional structures, the author sets out with the analysis of the changes in the working status of women who were mostly engaged in agriculture in a village that was fast losing agriculture as a primary occupation. As she moves from the first survey to the last in the thirty-year span, the land under cultivation in the village shrinks drastically from 1973 acres in 1979-80 to 926 acres in 1995-96 to just 349 acres in 2009-10, by which time the area of land under plotted house-sites became much larger than the land under cultivation, and of course, the fallow land in the hands of speculators or framers speculating on their own lands for higher prices, was much more than the plotted sites. When the first survey was done in 1979 almost all the village land of about two thousand acres was under cultivation of which more than half the cultivation was under irrigation with highly female labour intensive paddy as the main crop. There was hardly any mechanization, and almost all the women workers were engaged in agriculture except a few in the additional supplementary employment as helpers in activities like pottery, and cleaning and spinning of wool. It was almost completely agricultural work in which women were engaged as self-employed non-wage workers or wage employed agricultural labourers. With the beginning of 1980s, and with the entry of industrial activity in the region, there were fast changes in the land and labour relations in the village with adverse impact on female employment. Acquisition of part of the land for industrial activity sparked off drastic changes in the land use and landholding structure. From the scenario of the past with almost unchanging erstwhile land relations and insignificant market for land, there emerged an active land market, steep rise in land values, and increasing diversion of agricultural land for non-agricultural uses, which the author describes in detail as a process of 'commodification of land'. The land under agriculture in the village declined from a situation of almost hundred percent in 1979, to less than half in 1995-96, and by 2009-10, only less than one-fifth of the land was available for cultivation. The diversion of land for non-agricultural activities, the decline of labour absorption in agriculture, and the increase in the labour redundant in agriculture were, paradoxically, followed by increase in wages because of rising prices and other external influences. The result was, even as the size of agricultural holdings were tending to be increasingly small and marginal, there was deployment of labour saving machinery in agriculture and change in the cropping pattern away from more labour using crops like paddy. These changes had direct impact on the labour market, and particularly, there was a steep decline in female employment. In the case of male workers, some of those who were displaced from agriculture were provided some skill training and absorbed in industry, some turned to self-employment in transport and trade activities and yet others got into speculative activities. But there were hardly any alternative choices for female workers displaced from agriculture. In addition to loss of agricultural work, women also lost their traditional non-farm activities like pottery, cleaning and spinning of wool for making cottage woolen blankets etc. because of disappearing of markets for these products which were displaced by modern factory made substitutes. In the case of male oriented rural non-farm activities like carpentry, laundry, hair dressing etc. men could retain the skill and move to provide these services for which demand was rising in urban areas. But women agricultural workers hardly had any alternative skills, and most of them were not educated to be trained for any industrial skills. Nor were they ready for menial jobs which did not afford them the dignity that work in agriculture gave. The result was that most of the female workers displaced from agriculture ended up in domestic work, which is presented as a process of 'housewifisation' of erstwhile productive female workers. Interestingly, there was also certain 'feminization' of agriculture, because even though there was decline in the total employment in agriculture, the relative share of women increased, since the rate of decline in women's employment was less than that of men, many of whom moved to non-agricultural activities. The worst affected among the female workers were those belonging to female-headed households. While wage workers were left without any alternative work, the self-employed members of female-headed households were targeted for harassment and threats, by the growing groups speculators, with the ulterior motive of appropriating the landed property of these highly vulnerable households.

The study was also extended, by way of a case study, to analyse the conditions of female employment in a large steel and engineering factory in the neighbourhood of the village. What came out was that much of the female employment in the factory was confined to one division namely, the Engineering Component Division (ECD). This was a highly automated component production unit where the supervisor would calibrate the machine and the female workers' job was confined to collecting and stacking of the components—a routine work. There was actually much of deskilling that took place here rather than any training provided to the female employees. There was no women in supervisory capacity. Moreover, very few women from the village were employed here, the preference was for younger migrant women workers mostly informally employed without any employment or social security, and they were recruited either through labour contractors or informal contacts or senior workers related to them. Low wages and insecurity were the basic characteristics of these female workers.

In this bleak and deteriorating employment opportunities for women, one of the initiatives by the state to promote self-employment opportunities for women was the Swarnajayanti Gram Swarojgar Yojana (SGSY). The study, by undertaking a field survey of the Self Help Groups (SHGs) in the village makes an assessment of the impact of the programme in providing productive self-employment to women. The results show that while the state sponsored bank-linked SHGs did provide modest loan facilities to the SHG households, it helped more to soothen their consumption needs, and only about one-fourth of the women of the SHGs could take to income generating activities (IGAs). But more revealing is the detailed analysis of the commercial for-profit micro-finance institutions (MFIs) that mushroomed in the state beginning with early 2000s. At the behest of global finance capital many of the non-governmental organization (NGOs) which were functioning as charitable non-profit organizations were prompted to enter micro-finance business of providing credit to women's groups. The study, on the basis of detailed evidence collected on the nature of lending practices followed by some of these MFIs, shows that their interest charges amounted to as high as 74 percent and there were multiple agencies lending to the same household which often resulted in unredeemable debt burden forcing some of the borrowers to resort to the extreme action of committing suicide.

The study is much more exhaustive than the sketchy description provided above. It brings back the classical question of transition as a critical phase in the development process which is bound to displace several traditional activities and thereby rendering large section of working population highly vulnerable to displacement. And of all the sections of workers, as the available evidence clearly suggests, women in traditional occupations including agriculture are likely to be severely affected by the process. There are no coping mechanisms for them to be reintegrated into the productive livelihood activities that would ensure better living conditions, and to that extent impacting their economic status. One of the major challenges before any civilized society is to design appropriate measures of intervention by the state to smoothen the adverse impact of the process. The neoliberal facilitator state is bound to render the transition process precarious for a large proportion of women workers due to failure to intervene by designing appropriate measures to reintegrate them in the productive economic activities.

It must be said that scope of the work is apparently

ambitious. It appears so largely because of the undesirable trend that has penetrated development studies where all development is reduced to poverty studies, denuding the complexity of the processes. And this disorientation has distorted development studies and detached it from the task of abstraction of complexities of processes and presentating them as meaningful explanations. True, such abstractions and explanations are difficult to handle, as could be seen from the present study. The effort in this study could be seen more as labour of commitment, often defying the conventional method that calls for rigour. For those who follow the text as it is presented, it may be a difficult read. But for those who read it with questions in their mind, as any student of development should, the book is a rewarding reading in development studies.

D. Narasimha Reddy
Professor of Economics (Rtd.)
University of Hyderabad

Acknowledgements

The author wishes to acknowledge and thank the Indian Council for Social Science Research (ICSSR) for providing financial assistance for completion of this work. I am most grateful to Prof. R. Radha Krishna who has been the spirit behind in motivation for this work right from writing of the proposal to completion of the report. He always evinced a keen interest despite his busy schedule. I am equally thankful to Prof. D. Narasimha Reddy who has given adivse whenever I sought for it and also for writing the foreword which in painstaking and provided a critical assessment and relevance of the work. I am thankful to Prof. S.N. Sangeetha, I SEC, Bangalore for his help in arranging a research scholor, I am thankful to Prof. G. Haragopal for offering valuable suggestions at different stages of the work. My thanks are due to: Prof. Sheik Galab, the Director, Centre for Economic and Social Studies for his cordial cooperation in my endevours, I am thankful to Dr. Y. Venugopal Reddy, Former Governor Reserve Bank of India who has gone through the drafts of the work and advised me to send it to Mrs. Usha Thorat for her comments. I am beholden to Prof. Abdul Aziz, visiting professor at National Law University Bangalore, who took the pains to go through the work meticulously and helped to improve the overall frame of this work to Prof. B. Sambi Reddy for his help in all statistical applications and to Prof. C.H. Balaramulu for his support in fieldwork.

I also express my thanks to Prof. Gopinath Reddy, Prof.

Padmanabha Rao, Mr. K. Venkatiah at CESS, for their continuous help.

I am thankful to Dr. G. Vijay, Assistant Professor, University of Hyderabad, Hyderabad, who has been of great help in advising and collecting relevant books, and my daughter-in-law Dr. M. Krishnaveni and my special thanks are due to two grand daughters Khushi Kriti and Sindhu Anandi who provided a cordial climate at home that helped in the completion of my work.

The CESS librarian Mr. Simhachalam and his staff have always shown keenness in locating the required material. The office particularly Mrs. Lucy, Vani and Sharma made my accounts hassle free. Mr. Sree Hari's efficient and forthcoming help was always available for computer services. I am thankful to Mr. Edaiah for his patience in processing the data. I am thankful to Mrs. Shashikala, National Law University Bangalore for her assistance whenever it was needed.

I am grateful to Mr. Suresh Kumar, the Collector Medak District who made collection of data smooth, Mr. Subbaiah Choudhari, Commissioner, Customs and Central Excise enabled me to have access to industry. I also place on record my appreciation to the management of Pennar industry in providing access to respondents and paid attention to the research team. I am thankful to Mr. Vasanth Sharma, Mr. Bhaskar Rao whom I have approached several times for discussions and clarifications and Mr. Asaiah who took us to the houses we required to visit in our fieldwork. I am thankful to the SHG women for allowing us to attend their meetings. This work is a collective product of many people and organizations and their goodwill.

Overview

This study is on agrarian transition[1] of a semi-arid, paddy cultivating Telangana village. The agrarian transition among other things involves a shift of labour from agriculture to non-agriculture in search of better conditions. The focus of this study is to probe into the quality of life and work life in the occupations of female labour shifted from female intensive, sex sequential paddy cultivation to non-agricultural occupations. The initiation of agrarian transition in the village under study is traced with the introduction of commercialization of paddy cultivation. The state was instrumental in initiating commercial[2] agriculture under the guidelines of the Ford Foundation in the late 1970s. To encourage the commercialization of paddy cultivation the state extended support of the welfare schemes and bore-well technology to expand paddy crop. The commercialization of paddy had enjoyed the access to the financial support from the joint family household members who entered into public sector industries launched for the development of this backward region for *Garibi Hatao* (political agenda of Indira Gandhi) during the same period. These two state interventions to start with (support for commercialization of paddy and industrialization) triggered female farm employment. The expansion in female employment was achieved with the increase in area that shifted from various sources like Government Commons, land from dry crops with low female labour intensive to paddy (with bore-wells). The expansion in area along with application of new technology raised intensity of the paddy crop resulting in rapid rise in crop productivity and incomes from paddy crop.

The expansionary phase of female farm employment on paddy cultivation could not last longer. The rising incomes of the farm households initiated a process of the 'housewifization' that resulted in the withdrawal of women from hired agricultural work as a symbol of self-esteem of the family. Such effects were followed by the subsequent market-centric (new policy), deregulated macro agricultural and industrial policies. They pushed the well performing agriculture into a downward spiral. This spiral started with upward *coil* of the input prices and downward spiral of output prices resulting in the non-remunerative sales for crop produce of the farmers. These conditions were further worsened with the enactment of the Special Economic Zones (SEZ) policy in 2005 which shot up the land prices to result in mass speculative real estate business in the land market. This is followed by the change in role of the state from its earlier role of welfare in the new market economy. This resulted in withdrawal of state support from building the farm infrastructure, development of irrigation and its maintenance[3] (Annexure 2, for natural irrigational sources that were active up to the early 1980s). Added to infrastructural difficulty, the input package of commercialization (under the Green Revolution (GR) technology[4]) like seed-fertilizers, use of tractors and pesticides turned unaffordable without state support and pushed the cultivation into unviable occupation, particularly for small and marginal paddy cultivators. These macro policy changes in agriculture sparked an upward spiral of distress in the cultivation of paddy crop (that was developed under bore-well technology) particularly for the small and marginal farmers. Along with these unaffordable input costs and stagnant infrastructural development these farmers experienced a drastic fall in the supply of arable land[5] pushing paddy cultivation to a putdown occupation. These series of changes have been displacing female labour from land and forced to enter non-farm livelihood occupations. A significant number of female labour were affected with these change processes because of the given nature of land distribution in the village.

The small and marginal farmers far exceeded in number with a distribution of 97 and 98 per cent of one to two acres of wetland forming more than 70 per cent cultivators in the village. Therefore the distress hit a large section of the farming community affecting a major part of the village economy and female employment.

The market-centric model hit simultaneously the second source of support that agriculture enjoyed till the late 1980s. The public sector undertakings lost their priority with change in the macro-economic policy which otherwise provided financial support to agriculture.[6] The same policy change also led to division of joint families resulting in further fragmentation of land holding (to the extent of more than 54 per cent) and triggered land disputes by 1999. This policy created new opportunities of work in industries for young educated female workers that got unskilled in agricultural skills and had to shift to non-farm industrial employment. The forced shift of older generation (as has been witnessed) from farm occupations along with the younger generation caused an acute shortage in female agricultural labour. Such significant changes in livelihood asset distribution, occupations and skills have led to the changes in production roles of female farm labour (that they were doing earlier). This change in production roles affected not only those who still continued farm production on left-over scanty farm but those who shifted to the non-farm livelihood occupations in the village. To understand the changes in production roles of female labour the processes of change in the distribution of livelihood assets need to be probed.

By 2009-10 the number of small and marginal cultivators that survived in cultivation got reduced to 15 per cent of households compared to 80 per cent in the late 1970s. The holding size fell to 1/4th of land per-household in 2009-10 to the size prevalent in 1999. With such drastic fall both in the area of cultivation and in number of viable holdings, the farmers were compelled to resort to strategies that reduced the costs on cultivation to convert their holdings viable. The new strategies included methods like re-arranging land holdings, limiting the cultivation to family members, reorganizing the family farm activities (mechanized and manual), reallocating the intra-household division of farm works, re-mobilizing resources and relocating the product markets and restructuring the cropping patterns between food and commercial crops or sliding down to low investment crops.

The adoption of these new strategies resulted in new female labour production forms like- *female family farm labour (unpaid labour), feminized farm labour (by sliding down to low investment crops), pluri-activity female labour*[7] *and female hired agricultural labour and new female farm activities (previously they were done either by male labour or by machine).* It is significant to observe that these cost reduction strategies adopted by small and marginal farmers to turn their unviable farm holdings into viable have affected female production roles along with the change processes adopted by the wage-dependent cultivators that were working for cost-effective strategies. These cultivators consolidated resources like land and water and caused dualistic changes in the roles along with the social composition of land ownership.

The cost-saving strategies of marginal and small farmers included enlargement of family farm holdings to engage family labour fully. While the cost-effective strategies of wage-dependent cultivators either commercialized land into orchids, or shifting the cultivation to other villages. These dual strategies adopted by the two categories of cultivators changed the social composition of ownership of land. The small farmers' households that were near-land-less and depended either on female hired wage labour or tenancy cultivation during the last 30 years have purchased small pieces of land to increase their farm land to engage family female labour fully. Against this section, the wage-dependent cultivators lost considerable area of land to business and fell to a low level compared to what they enjoyed during the last thirty years. This paved the way to loss of land-based power.

The land-based power or the power that was exercised by upper caste and class in the village got diluted with the change in social composition of land ownership. The monopoly over the Sarpanch position held by the landed gentry for the last thirty years was upset with the enactment of the 73rd amendment that enforced reservation. The Sarpanch position went to backward castes (BCs) for the first time in the history of the village. Such a transition has weakened the power of the erstwhile landed rich. In essence increasing power of the 'capital' accentuated the agricultural crisis as the role of the rural elite has been declining in policy choices. For instance, the land rich remained mere spectators when the capital created acute shortage of agricultural labour by diverting the village labour under NREGP to work for corporate contractors facilitated by the state.

To capture experiences of cultivators from various classes, castes and gender, the study presents a number of case studies. The study also presents a focused group discussion of women that throws light on the changes in the intra-household gender relations with change in production roles. This study covers a broad range of issues of transition not only in the farm sector but in the non-farm sector. The non-farm occupations associated with agriculture as cash-generating production roles are dealt with. One of the new non-farm livelihood occupations under 'New paradigm of development' targeting women, through Self-Help Groups (SHG) were initiated by the state for poverty alleviation and their empowerment is enquired into. For this purpose a case study on village SHGs and its growth from its birth is studied with illustrations of respondents' cases.

The modern non-farm occupations in the village are discussed at two levels. At one level the new non-farm occupations that excluded women's role in production and industries that included young educated female labour from the village at another level. The non-farm industrial work opportunities for those female labour that are migrated for industrial employment are dealt with. To study this non-farm employment a case study is done on a new manufacturing industry. The case study focuses on the changes in employment and the quality of work life of women in non-farm employment. The case study is included in Section II of this report. This overall study attempts to capture a comprehensive picture of transition of occupational mobility in farm and occupational shifts into non-farm in the neo-liberalized model of development.

NOTES

1. Agrarian transition among other things involves a shift of labour from agriculture to non-agriculture. Bina Agarwal, a gendered agrarian transition, *Journal of Agrarian Change*, Vol. 3, No. 172, January-April 2003
2. The commercialization of crops implies production for market and for earning cash incomes. The access to land is increasingly facilitated through market transactions through purchase or rent and more generally the farm inputs and outputs are increasingly mobilized and valorized through market relations. The commercialization focuses on the various ways in which exchange values as opposed to use values assuming growing significance in the organization of economic and social life.
3. In 1992 both the Khusro Committee and Narsimhan Committee have observed that the agricultural sector need not be considered as a priority sector for the loans from the commercial banks. This resulted in closure of several rural banks. With enactment of this recommendations from 1991 the seed sector is permitted 100% share in the subsidies and subsidies on fertilizers are reduced.
4. Green Revolution technology is a large-scale application of science and technology for rural transformation, Package (package refers to ideology and programme). A launching pad for rural industrialization (Dhanagare, 1987, GR and Social Inequalities *EPW*, Vol. 22, No. 19/21 May Annual Number).
5. The drastic fall in cultivable land was due to the following reasons; a significant portion 57 per cent of farm land sales shifted it to non-farm due to both physical and financial constraints for cultivation in the new market, the supply of land further fell on account of state acquisition for launching of public sector undertakings that has attracted the real estate business. The

supply of land for cultivation also fell due to withdrawl of the share-cropping by land rich households when the policy of direct-loans-to-tenants was enacted by the state. The farm land that engaged wage labour fell due to diversification of crops into orchids and consequently land got concentrated and consolidated to facilitate use of mechanization. The farm land fell due to the fact that they shifted a part of their cultivation from the village to other neighbouring villages. The land supply also affected adversely when more than 1/3 of the cultivators kept their holdings fallow. Thus the high unaffordable cost of inputs, unsustained agricultural infrastructure and shrinking supply of land resulted increasingly in unviable cultivation particularly of the small farmers.

6. The State announced a "liberalized State Incentive Scheme" in 1989 and a "General Incentive Scheme" in 1992 for setting up "new industries" under the liberalization policy. According to these policies, a new industry unit located in "export promotion zone" is eligible for 15-20 per cent of subsidy on fixed capital investment. Under the "new comprehensive incentive scheme" an additional five per cent of subsidy is provided to the industries started in industrial estates. Seventy-five per cent of sales tax deferment is announced for a 10-year period for large and medium-scale industries. Interest rate on loans is announced as 6 per cent, power rebates 25 per cent, depreciation limits were enhanced. Many such other incentives were added.
7. The survival strategy of this class is based on Pluri-activity. This means men undertake off-farm work and women work on the farm.

1

Scope, Methodology and Three Surveys

The main objective of the study is to trace the relationship between the processes of commoditization of farm land and the changing female production roles in farm employment. To track occupational shifts from farm to non-farm and examine the changes in quality of work life. To trace new *social structures of accumulation* emerging in the processes of new female non-farm employment. To explore the trajectory of intra and inter-farm, non-farm and policy impacts on female employment.

Chapterization: This study starts with a brief introduction followed by seven chapters. Chapter I deals with the introduction and the socio-economic conditions in Medak district and also Patancheru Mandal and the village under study. This chapter presents the first, second and third household surveys done in previous and present decades in 1979-80, 1995-96 and in 2009-10. Chapter II deals with the survey of literature followed by the critical analysis of three surveys presented in Chapter I. Chapter III discusses the strategies of sustenance on land on the non-farm activities, both traditional and modern. Chapter IV presents case studies to see the impact of changes on class, caste and gender. Chapter V deals with Self-Help Groups and Micro Enterprises set by SHG members in the village. Chapter VI deals with a manufacturing industry. Chapter VII presents the conclusions of this study.

Methodology: This village study made use of multiple research methods with specific interview schedules. Separate interview schedules were structured to interview cultivator households (with a separate space for male and female). The interviews with the sample households were held in three phases coinciding with three seasons of agriculture. Each season has a slot of three months. The first slot survey was done in the months of July, August, and September, the second slot spreads over October, November and December and the last slot includes January, February and March. The study in three slots provides an opportunity to observe shifts in female employment in all agricultural seasons.

The working of tenancy and MGNREGP labour are dealt with in separate schedules.

A separate interview schedule is developed to interview the women respondents from Self-Help Groups. Another interview schedule is structured to elicit information from the women who have set up the micro-enterprises from these Self-Help Groups.

A separate interview schedule is prepared orienting the male and female workers working in the Engineering Component Division of the new manufacturing industry (PENNAR) with a focus on quality of work life.

For the officials from Gram Panchayat, people's representatives, patwari and chairman of agricultural co-operative credit society, officials from Indra Kranthi Patham (IKP), General Manager HRD, from the Pennar manufacturing industry, and manager from the Industrial Infrastructure Corporation of Patancheru Mandal separate schedules were designed.

The other methods like the focused group discussions, participant observation method and the case study method are used to capture the quality of life and work life of female labour. This study is based on sample surveys. The following methods are adopted for sample selection.

Sampling Method Used: The data on the farm details of the households are collected based on **multi-stage stratified sampling procedure** which is applied for the selection of sample in (2009-10). For selection of a representative sample of the households the first stage of stratification was based on the selection of Blocks (sub-village) recorded by the Gram Panchayat Office. The Gram Panchayat Office recorded the village (old) households in six blocks. These are the blocks in which the old households that were covered for the other two surveys in 1979 and 1995-96 staid. Two new blocks that developed into business centres are excluded for the study.

The second stage of stratification applied to the household from the above selected blocks is based on land. The stratification of the households included landed and landless households. Out of the total landed, a sample of 38 households who have sown the farm land in 2009-10 were selected and carried interviews with males and females separately.

These sample households are stratified into the social categories like ST, SC, BC and FC. Table (A) provides information on the stratifications of landed households.

Table A: Total Households Stratified into Landed and Landless in Village in 2009-10

	Scheduled Tribes	*Scheduled Castes*	*Backward Classes*	*Other Castes*	*Total*
Landed Hh	Nil	45	116	40	201
Landless Hh	3	34	68	38	143
Total	3	79	184	78	344

Source: Village record (2009-10)

Details of households included (sub-castes in SCs mala and madiga), while among BCs 16 sub castes), and among FCs (sub castes) noted in the village.

hh denotes households.

The landless households are stratified based on value of the house assets owned by them. The details on house assets are collected from the Gram Panchayat records to categorize them into slab-roofed houses, tile-roofed houses and tin-roofed houses. Weightage system is used for multiple houses owned by a single household. These values are grouped in-high, medium and low value houses to select a representative sample. The selected representative sample households are stratified into occupational and social categories for the study.

For the study on SHGs a random purposive sample of 91 respondents were drawn out of a total of 65 groups in the village during 2009-10. The representative sample drawn is based on two-tier stratification of the members. The first tier stratification is based on occupations in which SHG members are engaged. The second tier of stratification is based on the social category. The women groups are engaged mainly in 10 types of occupations in the village (Q. No. 1.4). The sample selected from them is as follows.

Q. No. 1.4: Main Occupations of the SHG Respondents

Main Occupation			*Caste*		
	ST	*SC*	*BC*	*OC*	*Total*
Own agriculture	0	2	0	0	2
Housewife	1	11	16	7	35
Government employee	1	2	0	1	4
Industrial contract worker	0	2	3	1	6
Unskilled business	0	1	8	3	12
Tailor	0	3	7	5	15
Sari rolling	0	0	1	1	2
Construction worker	1	3	7	0	11
Non-agricultural labour	0	0	1	1	2
Agricultural labour	0	1	0	0	1
Dhobi	0	0	1	0	1
Total	3	25	44	19	91

The social stratification of the sample members shows that three respondents are selected from scheduled tribes (STs), 25 are from scheduled castes (SCs), 44 were from backward castes (BCs) and 19 respondents were drawn from forward castes (OCs) for the study.

The study also elicited data on the employment and purpose of loan spent for the rest of the SHG group members (other than respondents) of the sample groups.[1]

Out of these groups case studies are selected based on source of funds. A sample of two case studies from SGSY groups, a case study of the village (under study) IKP groups. Four case studies are covered from IKP groups. Two case studies are covered from pavala vaddy groups and two more case studies are covered from corporate private microfinance groups. The following Table (B) shows sample data for all three research sites of the village.

Table B: Sample Covered for the Three Sites of the Village Study in 2009-10

Caste	*Agriculture Hh sown*			*Industrial Workers from Village in Nos*			*SHGs*
		1			*2*		*3*
	Male	*Female*	*Total Respondents*	*Male*	*Female*	*Total*	*Female in Nos.*
ST	1	1	2	Nil	Nil	Nil	3
SC	9	9	18	11	2	13	25
BC	22	23	45	43	5	48	44
OC	4	5	9	23	1	24	19
Total	36	38	74	77	8	85	91

The study on SHGs cover female domestic labour, as many of them are housewives.

A Case Study on a Manufacturing Industry. Pennar is selected (in 2009-10) as it employs maximum number of female labour among all industries in the Patancheru Industrial Estate. The Pennar employed female labour only in the Engineering Component Division. A sample of both males and females working in the first shift was selected. A purposive random, stratified sample in three tiers is adopted for selection. The first tier is based on gender stratification. Seven male and 27 female workers were drawn out of total 25 males and 60 female workers in the Hydraulics division in the first shift (Table C).

Table C. Sample Selected from ECD Department

	Male	*Female*	*Total*
ST	1	0	1
SC	1	3	4
BC	3	15	18
OC	2	9	11
Total	7(28%)	27(45%)	34 (40%)

The second tier of selection is based on level of employment. From the cadre of junior staff three male and 19 female workers, from the contract cadre two male and seven female workers and from casual cadre one worker from each gender is drawn (see Table D). This sample selected works out to more than 45% of female workers of the division.

The third tier of these selected are stratified in social categories (see Table D). It comprises one STs, four SCs, 18 BCs and 10 OCs.

Table D. The Sample Selected from ECD

	Total Workers (in one shift)	*Sample out of Total*				
		Permanent	*Staff*	*Contract*	*Casual*	*Total*
No. of males	25	1	3	2	1	7
No. females	60	0	19	7	1	27
Total	85	1	22	9	2	34

Note: The permanent worker is the male manager.

The production operators and quality controllers have also been included in the sample. The manager of the ECD has been interviewed.

The second shift also constitutes the same number of male and female workers. This facilitates for projection of results to 2/3 workers. However, in the third shift only male workers are employed and is not included in the sample.

The data on the manufacturing industry for the previous year is drawn from the case study done in the year 1999 on BPL formal, engineering industry that employed young educated girls in its informal division on automated machines. As this industry was closed, the study is conducted on the Pennar industry which has similar working conditions of female labour and therefore comparable.

These sample respondents selected from all the above studies are placed under social categories.

Source for the Secondary Data: The secondary data relating to the last two decades is drawn by the scholar's own work[2]. The secondary data is also collected from various libraries in New Delhi (Teen Murti), Bengaluru, Hyderabad and from ICSSR in North East Hill University Shillong. It also includes the official documents from District Planning Division (Medak), state level Bureau of Economics and Statistics, Mandal Development Office and Gram Panchayat Office. Both published and unpublished data are tapped for this research. Some of the research methods such as Case Study Method, Focused Group Discussion and Participant Observation Method are important in capturing various complexities of transformation of the village economy.

Importance of Case Study Method: Case study is crucial to capture the complexities of transformation, to raise new questions and analyse continuities and changes. However the case study on the village has gone a step further to examine the issues of changes that have affected and being affected by the related sectors (sites). The limitations of the macro level data based on traditional classification may not reveal the nuances and implications of local transformation that is vitally linked to political manoeuvres. They conceal significant information. This case study, it is hoped, will contribute to policy making. However, it cannot be generalized as it refers to a specific region.

The case studies covered here help in highlighting female specific problems encountered in cultivation/or in the labour market or in the financial market and in industry. It presents various problems of socio-economic life and the problems with state policies like tenancy and MGNREGP. The case study on Self-Help Groups brings out the quality of so-called potential employment for women in micro enterprises. These studies are done across the castes and classes. All these case studies are expected to provide deeper insights into the nature of transition.

Participant Observation: There are several areas that are sensitive to ascertain data with the interview schedule. To overcome such problems this method is useful. This was possible as the author studied in the village school and has access to proper persons who can provide reliable data. For a socio-economic understanding of the rural Medak, the District, Mandal and village historical profiles are presented.

Socio Economic Conditions and the Property Relations in the District of "Methuku Seema": The history of Medak district in Andhra Pradesh shows that it was under the *Zamindari* system[3] that was abolished in the 1950s. It is also a semi-arid region. (this means—unpredictable weather, limited erratic rains, nutrient poor soil and degraded land). In 1987 the Telugudesam government reorganized administrative divisions in the district and renamed the then existing taluques as Mandals. Even today there are 1265 revenue villages and 45 Mandals in this district and placed at 11th place in development ranking. In rural poverty Medak ranked 6th place as 22 per cent of its population was poor. The gap between male and female literacy is striking with 36.98 of male literates and a mere 15.73 per cent of females literates. In female literacy it ranked 21 out of 24 districts in the state.[4]

The District has huge scope for additional arable land for expansion of cultivation on account of "Surfe Khas" lands, the land reserved for the Nizam's personal use which was passed on to the government. The distribution of cultivable land was supplemented with the development of semi-arid technology[5] by establishing 'ICRISAT' (an international crops research institute from semi and tropics under CGIAR). With these developments there was a shift of considerable amount of land that was under dry food crops like bajra, ragi, sorghum into paddy in the early 1980s with the expansion of bore-wells. During this period the state launched heavy industries in the district. The heavy investments, liberal subsidies and incentives were allotted by the state both in terms of finance and land assets under the industrial policy of "the development of the backward regions" for attaining the "commanding heights"[6] by the public sector industries. The industrialization has grown to a gigantic level in this region, which was supposed to be one of the biggest in Asia.

One can classify the nature of growth of these industries in two phases, in the first phase from 1965 to 1980 industries such as the Bharat Heavy Electrical Ltd (BHEL) a public sector undertaking with several ancillaries in the private sector was set up. The region developed planned ancillaries that are dependent on the public sector for marketing its products and developed into an industrial estate. The public sector undertakings like Allwyn Watch Company, AP Scooters, Bharat Drugs Limited (BDL) and Oil and Detonators Limited (ODL) were established in the public sector. There were altogether 372 heavy and large-scale industries and 4,503 medium and small-scale industries located in this industrial estate. These industries to start with could expand formal employment in the region which helped the people to improve and pursue both cultivation and formal employment. Both farm and non-farm (sectors) worked as mutually dependent sectors within a joint family set up (Annexure 4). The district had all favourable conditions for promotion of cultivation as additional land (from Surfekhas) was available, technology was developed for achieving higher yields and capital could be accessed for investment from both formal and informal sources. The formal source being nationalized banks. The informal source is the salaries of the formal sector household members who joined the industrial employment from cultivator households. Along with these favourable conditions for cultivation water resources were also accessible. The water resources of the district are as follows.

The Manjeera- (tributary of Godavary river is a major source of water), the Haldee, Kudleru Peddavagu, Nallavagu waterfalls, Rainapally, Gangakathva, Narinja, Mogilipeta are sources for irrigation. In addition to these perennial sources, there were 6,207 irrigation tanks in the district for growing the main crop rice. In 1956 an area of 1,46,244 hectares of land was under cultivation under tanks. Under other irrigation sources like canals 1,416 hectares, under wells 31,800 hectares and under other sources 1,416 hectares were irrigated in the district. By 2007-08 the actual area irrigated was 15,930 hectares in kharif and 10,092 hectares in rabi (*Handbook of Statistics 2007-08*).

(Arrival of paddy to the district market stood at 14,42,065 quintals with a valoue of Rs 7,781.60 lakh).

Socio-Economic Conditions in the Mandal Patancheru: The data on employment on farm from rural Patancheru Mandal shows that it had 10.13 per cent of population as cultivators and 21.57 per cent as agricultural labourers during 2004-05 (*Statistical Handbook, 2004-05*). There were 3,948 male and 6,547 female agricultural labour in the ratio of 0.60:1. There were 3691 male and 1,239 female cultivators that works out to ratio 2:97. The non-farm sector engage 648 male and 585 female in the ratio 1:1.107 (*Statistical Handbook 2007-08*, Sanga Reddy). The major crop being paddy it engaged extensive female labour. The paddy cultivation used to cover 1,292 hectares in kharif and 389 hectares in the rabi season in Patancheru Mandal in 2007-08 (*Statistical Handbook, 2007-08*). However the data shows that by this time more than 29 per cent of land has been converted into current fallows in the Mandal. This indicates massive displacement of labour from paddy lands that effects female labour.[7]

The social composition of the Mandal shows that the SC population was 16,956 constituting 14.46 per cent of the population of the district. The percentage of literates among male SCs constituted 74.26 per cent and among SC female 54.16 per cent which is above the state's average (*Statistical Handbook 2004-05*, Medak district chief planning officer, Sanga Reddy). This could be because of educated migrants in search of industrial work. In this backdrop of the Mandal a series of the village surveys covering the socio-economic background over a period of three decades is presented as follows.

The Socio-economic Conditions of the Village: The First Household Survey (1979-80): The data on arable land in the village shows that there were many water resources for irrigation. The total irrigated land was 1,671.35 acres. Out of it 195.36 acres was under irrigation tanks, 31 acres was under other resources (kuntas), 75.11 acres was under backwaters of rivers and a mere 13 acres was cultivated with rain water (collected from the Gram Panchayat office) and the rest under wells. Out of 1,991 acres of land in the village 18 acres or which works out to less than one per cent was not under cultivation. The remaining 99 per cent of land was under cultivation and recorded as 'KABIL KASTU' meaning "fit for cultivation" up to the late 1950s. A major part of this area was under cultivation even up to 1984-85 (see Table 1).

This vast area of farm land under cultivation generated sufficient hired female labour. In the lean seasons traditional non-farm employment supplemented cash incomes for family. These occupations together made their tiny land holdings (annexure) economically viable for cultivation during this period. For this reason for more than 70 per cent of female labour from marginal and small farmer households, the farm land was the basic asset and agriculture was the main source of livelihood till the late 1980s. These farmer households were not willing to lose their source of livelihood. This made finding land for public sector industries a difficult task for the government. The land transactions were operated directly by the cultivators.[8] This is evident from the data in Table (1) that the land sales were very inelastic even up to the 1990s.

During the early 1980s (see Table 1) the total land under cultivation was 1,339 acres in the village under study (Vanamala, 2003). Out of it an amount of 160 acres or 11.94 per cent was sold in a period of about 20 years up to 1990-91. It is significant to note that out of the total land sold, about 50 per cent (75 acres) purchases were by cultivators of the same village. This reflects a deep desire for land for cultivation. From this it is clear that the peasants were not willing to sell the farm land. However, the state intervention initiated the shift of land from farm to non-farm in 1980-81. Out of this land the data in Table (1) shows that about 37 acres were acquired for setting up of industries in public sector. This acquired land works out to a mere 2.76 per cent of the total farm land. However this small fraction triggered the real estate business and buttressed the business of arable land for non-arable purposes. The land started moving away from the control of the villagers. This shift further picked up after the 1990s.

Table 1: Land Inelasticity in the Market

Year of Land Sale	*Total Land Sold*	*Industry*	*Land Sold to Real Estate*	*Agriculture*
1973-74	12.19	Nil	Nil	12.19
1974-75	11.13	Nil	Nil	11.13
1975-76	7.21	Nil	Nil	7.21
1976-77	9.29	Nil	Nil	9.29
1977-78	Nil	Nil	Nil	Nil
1978-79	13.02	Nil	13.02	Nil
1979-80	Nil	Nil	Nil	Nil
1980-81	32.52	6.25	26.27	Nil
1981-82	34.55	26.12	1.32	7.11
1982-83	Nil	Nil	Nil	Nil
1983-84	2.04	Nil	Nil	2.04
1984-85	4.01	Nil	Nil	4.01
1985-86	9.37	1.10	6.04	2.23
1986-87	Nil	Nil	Nil	Nil
1987-88	13.15	Nil	Nil	13.15
1988-89	8.03	Nil	1	7.03
1989-90	3.20	3.20	Nil	Nil
1990-91	0.34	Nil	0.34	Nil
Total	160.1	36.70	47.98	75.36

Source: Collected from MRO Office, Patancheru
Total land sales to= industry+ real estate+ agriculture= 160.1 acres (Col. 3+4+5)

After 1991 the second phase of industrialization took place under the policy of privatization, liberalization and globalization. The industries like BHEL fell under the non-priority sector, as private industries became the priority of the state policy[9]. The state turned out to be more a "broker" to acquire land for the private capitalists than public interest. The dispossession of farm land was followed by the processes of disappearances of traditional village non-farm employment. The base year is 1979 for the study in which the first survey was done.

The village under study is located on the banks of Nakkavagu, a perennial river. The other side of this river is

Patancheru the Mandal Headquarters.[10] The socio-economic surveys of the village focus on total working and non-working women; the social composition of the female farm labour, distribution of land and socio cultural practice of "housewifization".[11]

During 1979 there were 280 total households with total population of 906 in the village (Vanamala 1981). The male and female ratio was 1.08:1. The total farm land in the village was 1,333 acres and the farming was the occupation for 230 households (82%). The female labour constituted 67 per cent of the total in the working age group of female population. This explains that not less than two-thirds of the women were in the work force (Vanamala 1981). The paddy cultivation was the major activity in agriculture. Part of the wages for paddy were paid in kind. Therefore the female farm labour prioritized paddy cultivation over other labour activities to earn more paddy for family consumption. The landless and the near-landless households depended on agricultural wage work along with caste-based spinning, cane work, pot making and service activities like washing to earn supportive incomes (see Vanamala 1979). The social composition of working and non-working female labour is as follows.

The social composition of female labour in the working age group, the forward caste households constituted 22.5 per cent, from the backward castes 61 per cent and from the scheduled castes 16.5 per cent of the total population in the village (see Vanamala, 1979). The non-working women constituted 33 per cent in that age group. Among the women, the FC women were more in the non-working category (Vanamala, 1981 and 1982).[12] The children in the total population constituted 801 that worked out to the ratio of 1:1.34 of mother and children. This indicates the child care responsibility of working mothers along with their domestic labour and labour in production. 5-15 years age group constituted 37 per cent in the total population.

The composition of male and female hired agricultural labour constituted a mere 10.75 per cent of male and as high as 75 per cent of female hired labour from their respective working population in 1979 (Vanamala, 2003). This explains that the cultivation was female labour intensive and they were dependent on it for their livelihood. A majority of the female labour was hired labour along with labour on own land. Women's activities got diversified into hired, family labour and self-employed labour on rural non-farm activities. The family labour was more from FCs while the hired labour was more from SCs followed by BCs in that order. The female hired labour was earning cash incomes to contribute not only for family survival but also for earning capital for investments on their own small piece of land. The male labour mostly confined to the agriculture on own land. Against this widely labour absorbing paddy work the practice of "housewifization" has picked up as a status symbol in the wake of growing commercial cash incomes. The process of "housewifization" is seen in withdrawal of female from hired labour as and when male incomes were rising. It is important to note that this behaviour of the households is almost a universal phenomenon across the classes and castes but at various levels of economic status. This is also noticed at various levels of land and income across castes (Vanamala, 2003).

The analysis on caste and labour shows significant dimensions. About 72 per cent of the forward castes female workforce are working on their own fields while only 28 per cent of them accept hired work. From the backward castes 24 per cent of female workforce work on their own lands and 76 per cent of them accept hired work on others fields. From scheduled castes a mere 13 per cent of female workforce work on own land and 87 per cent work on hired labour. From this it is clear that lower the caste hierarchy, higher is the incidence of hired labour. This shows that higher the social status of the household more is the confinement of women for family work. This gets in the process of marginalization of female labour by not allowing them into hired labour. The following process explains the dynamics in the interaction between caste, land holding position and labour participation.

It is significant to note that in the land slab of 20.1 to 30 acres more than 71 per cent of women have not been working, while 100 per cent scheduled caste women were working in this land slab. (Vanamala, 2003) For this reason the maximum presence of workforce in the cultivation is from SCs followed by BCs. The hired and family female labour against land holding position across castes is as follows.

The forward caste women were not participating in hired work from land owned households above 10 acres. The backward castes and scheduled castes exhibit the same behaviour but after crossing ownership of 20 acres.[13] This explains that the marginalization of female labour is higher in the higher economic status of the households. The same behaviour is noticed in the interactions of caste and increase in income of the spouse.

It is observed that when the income of the husband goes up, he withdraws his spouse from hired labour and she gets confined to domestic activity within the house. For instance from the Rs 0-1,000 income per annum category of the household the female hired labour constitute as high as 88 per cent, while in the income category of above Rs 15,000 PA there were no female hired labour. This relationship of hired labour with caste and level of income reveal interesting results. From forward castes households there are no instances of hired labour after Rs 5,000 and above income PA while the hired labour was 100 per cent from these households where the income slab was Rs 1,000 and below PA (Vanamala, 2003). This data shows that the forward caste women were withdrawn from hired labour once the household crosses an income of Rs 5,000 PA. From the backward castes and scheduled castes, there was no hired labour after the household crossed Rs 10,000 and Rs 15,000 respectively (Vanamala, 1981).

These social practices are theorized by Maria Mies[14] as processes of "housewifization". She argues that money economy devalues "women's work" through this process of "housewifization" by creating "domestic work". She adds that the 'housework' or "domestic work" is nothing but appropriation of women's labour by not valuing it for income. With this understanding of socio-economic background of the village from the first survey, the second survey shows some noticeable changes in the village.

The Second Household Survey: The Socio-Economic Conditions of the Village (1995-96): The second household survey was done in 1995-96. The total population in the village was 5344 (socio-economic survey, MRO Patancheru and Vanamala Report 2003, p. 73). The male-female ratio has been 1.09:1. This ratio in the productive age group constitutes 1.57:1. Out of 533 households 206 were cultivator households. The total land available for cultivation was 926 acres (Socio-Economic Survey MRO Office Patancheru, 1995-06) (converted into dry) (see Table 2). This works out to 4.5 acres per capita per household (Vanamala 2003, Annexure 5). However the number of holdings in 1-2.5 acres constitute as high as 83 per cent of total holdings. The landholding size of 10.1 to 20 acres constituted mere 1.8 per cent of total holdings and it is under double cropped area. This explains that land distribution was qualitatively skewed and the larger area holders are small in number.

Table 2: Land Distribution (in acres) 1995-96

Land Slab	*Dry Land %*	*Irrigated Land 1%*	*Irrigated Land 2%*	*Total Land (dry)*
1-2.5.	386.00	225.00	152.00	763.00
	(69.90)	(94.95)	(97.5)	(82.39)
2.6-5	90.00	7.00	3.00	100.00
	(16.21)	(2.95)	(2.00)	(10.79)
5.1-10	37.00	5.00	00 00	42.00
	(6.70)	(2.10)		(4.55)
10.1-20	16.00	0.00 00	1.00	17.00
	(2.89)		(0.5)	(1.84)
20.1 & above	4.00	0.00 00	00 00	4.00
	(4.30)			(0.43)
Total	553.00	237	156.00	926.00
	(100.00)	(100.00)	(100.00)	(100.00)

Source: MRO Patancheru Socio-Economic Survey 1995-96. (Total land is standardized with 2 dry:1 wet)

(Irrigated land I and land II denote land under one crop and two crops respectively)

The distribution of irrigated land types I, II also shows that 95 and 98 per cent of it was owned in the size distribution of 1-2.5 acres (Table 2). This shows that irrigated land distribution was in a very large number of households. The ownership of wet holdings is very important from the point of view of employment for female labour.

In the subsequent higher level of the "small holdings" of 5-10 acres slab, the data shows that the land distribution was 42 acres that works out to about five per cent of cultivable land. From the next higher slab of 10 to 20 and above acres, the total land owned was dry and worked out to about two per cent of cultivable land. However this part (rich) of cultivators owned mostly dry land. These trends show that land distribution is skewed and owned by many peasants to whom it provides subsistence.

The occupational division of the female labour on land constitute 13 per cent on hired labour three per cent work on own land from the working female population during 1995-96 (Vanamala, Report 2003, Annexure 4). The female workers that work on their own farm land across the social categories constitute one per cent, four and three per cent from SC, BC, and from FCs respectively. While the female labour of the hired work category constitute 21 per cent from SCs, 18 per cent from BCs and 1.6 per cent from FCs out of the total female hired workers (Vanamla, 2003 report). It is very significant to note that the female labour possessed rural skills to work on non-farm occupations during this phase.

The rural non-farm occupations, mostly related to agriculture engaged about 25 per cent of total female workforce. It is also striking that those who are displaced from land could not find alternative non-farm work and had to remain as housewives. They constitute as high as 59 per cent of total female workers. The trend among the young males is different. Forty-seven per cent of them were trained in industrial skills (across castes) by 1995-96. It is significant to note that this not finding non-farm employment to female labour was in the context of availability of number of literate women as has been mentioned at the beginning of this chapter.

The percentage of literates among male SCs was 72 per cent and among female SCs 51.33 per cent during 1995-96 (Vanamala, Annexure 2, Report 2003). The literacy among BC males was 73 per cent and among females it was 52 per cent. The illiteracy among 'others' is a mere six per cent. Despite these educational levels, women did not have any training opportunities. With this socio-economic backdrop in 1995-96 the third survey shows these conditions in 2009-10 as follows:

The Third Household Survey: The Socio-Economic Conditions of the Village (2009-10):

The Gram Panchayat records show that there were 344 households in the village during 2009-10. Out of it 201 are landed and 143 are landless households. The social categories of the landed households show that a total of 37 households are from SCs, 128 from BCs and 36 from OC categories. The percentage of these households workout 18 per cent, 64 per cent and 18 per cent out of the total landed households (see Table 7). This explains that the BCs survive on land more, compared to the other two social categories. For such a dependence on cultivation, it is significant to note that the land that shifted to real estate plots (speculative business) constituted more than 426 acres (Table 3), that works out to 29 per cent area. This area exceeded much over that of land that is available for cultivation.[15] The land remained for cultivation was mere 349 acres (Table 3) that works out to 24 per cent of the total geographical area of the village in 2009-10.

Table 3: Total Geographical Area of the Village 2009-10

Status of Land	*Land*	
	in acres	%
Plots	426.13	29.3
Company	44.57	3.0
CPR (common property)	78.61	5.4
Houses	6.97	0.4
Irrigated	**349.25**	24.5
Padava	507.25	34.9
Unirrigated land	37.15	2.5
Total Land	1450.41	100.00

Source: Village revenue records

Table (4) and Table (5) shows that between 1995-96 and 2009-10 the dispossession of land for various reasons has been massive leaving an area of 220.35 acres or 17.69 per cent of total farm land of the village for cultivation.

Table 4: Dryland Distribution in 1995-96

Land Slabs in acres	*Land in acres*	*% of Land in each slab*
1–2.5	386	69.90
2.6–5	90	16.21
5.1–10	37	6.70
10.1–20	16	2.89
20 and above	4	4.30
Total	553	100.00

Source: MRO Patancheru Session 1995-96.

Table 5: The Dry Land Distribution in 2009-10

Land holding in acres	*Households Number*	*Percent-age*	*Area in acres*	*Percent-age*
Less than 1	110	55.6	21.09	9.6
1-2.5	64	32.3	95.06	43.1
2.6-5	17	8.6	58.20	26.4
5.1-10	7	3.5	46.00	20.9
10.1-20	Nil	0.0	00	0.0
Total	198	100.0	220.35	100.0

Source: Village revenue records

It is significant to note that not only is the total land under cultivation shrinking but also per cultivator holding size is shrinking over the years in both the dry and wet land holdings. Out of 198 dry landed households, 110 households are in the distribution category of less than one acre. This catagory of land slab was not there is 1995-96 (Table 4). The holding size also effected continuously 55.55 per cent households in tha land slab of less than one acre shared less than 10 per cent of land under cultivation (Table 5). In the land slab of one acre to five acres the percentage of cultivator households is 97 with a land share of 78 per cent of available dry land. The former land rich households that constitute four per cent of the total land, own about 21 per cent of land in the land slab of 5.1-10 acres. No households own any land in the higher slab beyond 10 acres as was the case in the previous survey. This explains that all cultivators including former landlords now own an area that falls under marginal and small farmers' category.

Table 6: Irrigated Land Distribution in 1995-96

Land slab in acress	*Wet land (1) in acress*	*Wet land (2) in acress*	*Total Land*
1–2.5	225.00	304	529
2.6–5	7.00	6	13
5.1–10	5.00	00	5
10.1–20	0.00	1.0	1
20.1 above	0.00	00	0
Total	237.00	311.00	548

Source: MRO Patancheru Socio Economic Survey 1995-96. Wet (II) Standardised with one acre wet (I) = 2 wet (II)

Table 6a: Distribution of Irrigated Land Holdings in 2009-10

Land (slab) in acres	*Number of Households*	*%*	*Area in acres*	*%*
+Less than 1	117	66.5	21.63	19.17
1-2.5	52	29.5	60.55	53.67
2.6-5	6	3.4	20.45	18.12
5.1-10	0	0.0	0	0.0
10.1-20	1	0.6	10.18	08.51
Grand Total	176	100.0	112.81	100.0

Source: Village revenue records.

The distribution of irrigated land (Table 6a) in 2009-10 shows that there are 67 per cent of households in the land slab of less than one acre with a share of about 20 per cent of total irrigated land available for cultivation. In the subsequent slab of 1-2.5 acres about 30 per cent of the households own 54 per cent of the total irrigated land. These two land slabs together constitutes 97 per cent of the households of the irrigated land holders.

Interestingly in the highest land slab of 10-20 acres, about 13 acres of irrigated land is owned by a single household. This is a new development and land got transferred to this household from other cultivators. In the entire history of the village, at no point of time this huge area of irrigated land was owned by any family. Such major changes in distribution of irrigated land across the social categories influence the village livelihoods enormously.

This land distribution across the social categories indicate the fact that a significant transition in the land ownership has taken place. The data on land distribution across social groups' shows among the BCs it has gone up compared to the area owned by this social category in 1995-96. This explains that the BC households particularly female labour that participate directly in land based labour have moved to family labour by purchasing land. (see Table 7). This can be explained to have done to reduce cost on cultivation that rose to an unprecedented level.

Table 7: Social Category-wise Number of Households Owning Land in 2009-10

Land slab	*SC*	*BC*	*FC*	*Total hh*
1-2 acres	19	67	12	98
2.6-5 acres	17	52.	17	86
Above 5 acres	1	9	7	17
Total hh	37 (18.40)	128 (63.68)	36 (17.91)	201

Sample survey done in 2009-10

The sample data suggests that about 64 per cent of existing land is owned by BCs (see Table 7). Most of them own the land in the land slabs of 1-2 acres and 2-5 acres in that order. This suggests that BCs moved towards family farm cultivation more than the other two categories. To depend on cultivation for livelihood the cultivator households restructured the cultivation along lines of the reduction in the cultivation costs to make their holdings viable by substituting family labour (Table 7).[1]

The viability of the holding is known with the income and expenditure of paddy cultivation.

The changes in the prices of market inputs of paddy cultivation, the interest burden on borrowings of crop loans and the progressive risk and burden of interest on the loans raised for bore wells (bw) digging (model 1) between the periods 1995-96 and 2009-10 shows an increase in production costs on paddy crop cultivation.

Cost of cultivation of paddy on one acre

Model 1		**1995-96**	**2009-10**
Male activities	*Wage/ Day/per labour* *1*	*Total Costs (Rs)* *2*	*Total Costs (Rs)* *3*
Ploughing			
Eirst and	200x2Lx1d	400	600
Second time	200x2Lx1d	400	600
Bunding	200wx3dx1L	600	900
Total		1400	2100
Harvesting			
Cutting	5Lx200wx1d	1000	1500
Kallam	5lx200wx1d	1000	1500
Grass	5lx200wx1d	1000	1500
Total	Call	3000	4500
Female activities			
Transplanting	12Lx100wx1d	1200ar S	2400
Weeding	8Lx100wx1d	800	1600
Second weeding	7Lx100wx1d	700	1400
Harvesting			
Cutting	5Lx100wx1d	500	1000
Grain collection	5Lx100wx1d	500	1000
Grass bundling	5Lx100wx1d	500	1000
Total		4200	8400
Costs on market inputs			
DAP	550x2(bags	1100	1200
Urea	90x2	180	1200
Tractor N	300x2hrs	600	1000
Pesticides	Nill		
Sprouts		300	500
Total		2180	3900
Grand total		10780	18900

l interest on cumulative crop loan of a hh	——cumulative		3834.77per hh interest burden
Interest on failed bore well loan of a hh	130'x40/ft=5,200	728	5,180

L—stands for labour; d—stands for days; w stands for wages

Model 1a. Changes in the Crop Productivity and Changes in the Market Prices

Changes	*1995-96*	*2009-10*
A. Productivity/acre	25	40
B. Cropped area in acres	95.24	120
C. Price per Quintal	Rs 700/Q	Rs 900/Q
Real gross per acre income at constant prices in 2009-10	Rs 17,500 per acre	Rs 28,000 per acre
Total production cost of paddy	Rs 11,508	Rs 18,900 per acre

The changes in the input costs of paddy production stated in (model 1 and 1a) affected the changes in the gross value of paddy crop, in current 1995-96 prices and in constant pricesas workedout. The costs of cultivation of paddy worked out to Rs 10780 in the year 1995-96 (see model 1). This shot up to Rs 18,900 by 2009-10. In addition to these input costs the per household interest burden on the cumulative crop loans stood at Rs 3834.77, (model 1, column 3) the number of failed bore wells (bw, and the interest risk on loans borrowed for bore well (bw) digging have been increasing progressively from Rs 728 per bore well in 1995-96 to Rs 5,180 per bore well by 2009-10. The data presented (model 1a) shows that the income of the peasants households affected with increase in the cropped area under paddy from 95.24 acres in 1995-96 to 120 acres in 2009-10, the productivity of paddy crop increased from 25 quintals per acre in 1995-96 to 40 quintals per acre in 2009-10. The third factor effected is the price of paddy that increased from Rs 700 per quintal to Rs 900 per quintal during this period. To understand the economic conditions of peasants the data on the expenditure and income earned have to be compared.

Based on this data the per acre real gross income at constant (prices table on model 1a) (in 1995-96 prices as base) works out to Rs 28,000 in 2009-10. This leaves a sum of Rs 2,61,100 aggregate net real income to the peasant households, which works out to Rs 7,252 real income per household per annum to the sample households. The bore-wells into which the cultivators have invested again by borrowings have been failing at an increased rate as the ground water table has been decreasing. Therefore the number of bore wells failed has been on increase. This has led to a situation as mentioned by the respondents that—where in, out of ten bore wells dug in 1995-96, two failed. This has increased to 5 failures in every 10 bore wells dug by 2009-10. The consequent result is that average cost of bw dug per household (hh) increased from Rs 5,200 (annexure table 8b) to Rs 37,000 by 2009-10. And this does not yet include the high interest rates on the loans borrowed to dig the bore wells. The interest worked out was Rs 728 on these loans in 1995-96, and gone up to Rs 5,180 in 2009-10 per bw (table 8a). As a proportion of the net real income it worked out to 0.5824 in 1995-96 and shot up to 13 per cent of the net real income of the household by 2009-10. The interest rates from all above sources including the institutional loans in general are very high (annexure table 8a). Added to these risks the problem of raising second crop in type two irrigated land also not that favorable to cultivators. The sample households having functioning bw go for second crop of paddy. The total area under second crop shows as 40acres and 30 guntas in the village. The costs of cultivation of this type 11 irrigated land being the same per acre like that of type 1 land, however the yield of this crop stands at $1/4^{th}$ of the first type land. This situations forced thepeasants to keep his small holdings fallow.

These cost and income conditions have lead to slide down of the households to lower levels in the distribution of incomes. This is evident from the data collected by MRO office on the distribution of income of the households of the village in 1995-96. The data is collected across the castes and classes that show that the households who were earning Rs 1,000 PA from cultivation were only nine in number in the village. this works out to (0.5 per cent) and the households that were earning an income of Rs 1,000-2,000 were also less consistuting 36 or (02 per cent) of households.

The households earning an income of Rs 2,001-5,000 per annum were 20 per cent. And 48 per cent of the households were earning an income of Rs 5,000-10,000 per annum. Another 18 per cent and 11 per cent of the households were earning an income of Rs 10,001-15,000 and 15,001-25,000 per annum. The income earning over Rs 30,000 per annum were two per cent (Socio-Economic Survey MRO Patancheru in 1995). On the whole 48 per cent of the villagers were in the average income slab of Rs 5,000-10,000 per annum. The poorest of the poor households were about 22 per cent in the village. Interestingly 53 per cent of the households from SC; 45 per cent of households from BCs and 50 per cent of households from FCs were in the average income slab of 5000-10000. The calculations of the real incomes (Table 7) corroborate with the calculations of expenditures (model 1) suggest that the real incomes earned by the cultivators in 1995-96 fell by 2009-10. The above data finds its significance in the review of literature of the scholars in the next chapter.

NOTES AND REFERENCES

1. Details of 91x12= 1092 members were collected for the study.
2. Vanamala (2003), "Impact of Industrialization on Female Employment" submitted to ICSSR.
3. States that did not have a history of landlordism have seen on average 23 per cent higher wheat yields. States which were historically under a landlord system have had significantly less public spending on health, education and agricultural technology in contrast to those that had the *Raiyatwari system*. Such regions witnessed lower infant mortality rate by 40 per cent lower than those that had the *zamindari* system. Ashok Kumar, Methukuseema charitra-samscruithy Manzeera Rachithala Sangham (2008).
4. the government set up a research institute in collabouration with USA called 'The International Council for Research and Investment in Semi-Arid Technology' ICRISAT) in the crops in short durations (HYV) in 1965.
5. Vanamala, ibid. (2003).

6. The state had created the Industrial Infrastructure Corporation of India (IICI), an institutional arrangement for development of infrastructure to industries and for purchase of land at market prices directly from farmers.
7. The chemicals and drugs, textiles, breviaries, spinning mills and the industries that were polluting water, land, air and food prevailed widely. Pollution control authorities became indifferent.
8. Ibid (14).
9. Maria Mies's theory of 'housewifization' describes the informal labour of women, providing a conceptual apparatus for understanding 'labours of love' and 'embodied' work that place the labourer herself, rather than her specific tasks, on the market. She claims that there is an intrinsic relationship between capitalism and patriarchy and that we can no longer accept a classical Marxist explanation of the capitalist system, because it does not include women. She goes on to propose that capitalism usurps the labour of women through a patriarchal system, which labels it as housework or subsistence work. In turn this "subsistence" work is not accounted for in the cost of labour (i.e. production), which leads to the accumulation of capital. This means that the labour of women is exploited by the system of capitalist-patriarchy, because it is not given credit for the economic benefits that it provides for the system. The authors complain, for instance, that the money economy devalues "women's work" through a process they call "housewifization" (in which women are made the guardians of this work). A cow for Hillary: Maria Mies and Veronika Bennholdt_Thomsen's "The Subsistence Perspective", Saturday, January 20, 2007 at 12:24 pm PST

   Also see Maria Mies "colonization and housewifization" caring labour an archive htt:/caring labour.wordpress.com2010
10. Vanamala (1982) Hired and Family Labor Among Women *Mainstream*, March 13.
11. These employees have withdrawn their working spouses immediately from farm work when their salary went up. With the implementation of SAP the compulsory voluntary retirement was imposed. Several such households went back to cultivation. In the next phase when they lost their jobs and joined the cultivation they could not provide re-entry for the spouse into agriculture. Because in social perception on this reentry into work reflects lowering of his esteem. This phenomenon is observed

even in the midst of significant modern developments in the region.

12. Maria Mies and Veronika Bennholdt-Thomsen's (2007)"The Subsistence Perspective", Saturday, January 20, at 12:24 pm PST NET
13. The land prices shot up with enactment of the SEZ Act that triggered the speculative land business resulting in shift to non-agricultural activities. The strategic land price bubble was also created for shifting the land from farm to non-farm to facilitate the undertaking of various heavy investment projects.
14. Unaffordable land prices did not allow cultivators to buy new land.

The annexure tables 8a and 8b shows the calculations of interest rates and rates of bore well digging annexure table 8a.

Annexure Table 8a. Crop Loans Raised by the Cultivator Households from the following Sources

	1@12% Co-operative society	*2@12% SBI/SBH*	*3@14% SHG*	*4@36% PRIVATE*	*Total*
	10000	60000	15000	2000	
	28000	62000	10000	2000	
	50000	20000	10000		
	8000	30000	6000	30000	
	60000		8000		
	60000				
	60000				
	Total 276000	172000	49000	34000	
Interest on these loan amounts in Rs	Rs 33120	I20640	I6860	12240=	72860
Per household burden in Rs					8064

Annexure Table 8b: Intensity of Risk in Bore-well digging

1995-96 cost of failed bw in Rs	2009-10cost of failed bw
Per 10 bore wells dug 2 failures	Per 10 bore wells dug, 5 failures
130′depth @Rs40/ft =5200/= cost of digging bw interest works out on this loan raised for digging failed bw(risk) risk=Rs728/@14% 728x14(failed)=Rs101.92/= (per bw interest risk)	100xRs55/ft =5500 rate of bore well digging+200xRs60/ft=12000+ +300xRs65/ft = 19500 total= 37000/ interest@14%=Rs5180 (for failed bw)

bw—à indicates bore well

Note: The rates for digging bore- wells: the market pattern of digging of bore-wells is that for First 100′ is dug at the rate of Rs 55 per feet followed by every subsequent feet up to 200′ is charged Rs 60 per feet, this is followed by Rs 70 for next 100′ this works out as 100 x 55- = 5,500 + 60 x 200 = 12,000 +300′ x 65 = 1,95,000; + 400′ x 70 = 28,000. = 65,000 this loan amount is very risky as the water content in the bore-well is uncertain. The depth of the bw has increased from 130′ in 1996-96 to 400′ in 2009-10

2

Three Decades of Development: Analysis of Land and Labour Relations

The three surveys done on the village with a time gap of one decade from 1979 to 2009-10, unfolds a series of changes in the production roles of female labour from farm to non-farm. The data shows that the dispossession of small holdings and consolidation of wage-dependent holdings resulted in displacement of female labour and shift to non-farm employment. This resettlement in non-farm is tracked for the quality of work-life. This completes the circuit of changes in production roles of female labour. For a proper analysis and understanding of this data the following review of the previous works on the subject, provides a framework.

Review of Literature: The studies on rural agrarian transformation with a focus on the reasons for dispossession of farm land, displacement of female labour and resettlement of this female labour in non-farm occupations and also impact of the state policies on employment and income of female labour in particular are examined. The following are the studies covering such concerns of female employment.

Michael Levien's[1] analysis shows that the agrarian transformation in India occurred through land speculation by rentiers who profited from artificially cheap land acquired by the state (Broker) mediation. Special Economic Zone is "hyper liberalized export enclaves" and is a legal way for private companies for accumulation of capital". He adds that this process from a long run perspective of dispossession of land and absorbing minimal labour from dispossessed- has created a pool of surplus labour that is more *marginalized than exploited*. He observes that this has contributed to widening inequalities between caste and class, undermining food security and fuelling *non-productive economic activity* which he characterizes as pre-capitalist form of exploitation. His analysis of the compensation received by the peasants for land acquired by the state enters into non-productive ways like *interest-based capital, petty mercantile capital or back into land, sharecropping and speculative real estate.* He observes that such pre-capitalist forms of exploitation do not add to productive transformation.

Sundaresan (2011)[2] in his analysis on land grabbing observes that land—the main source of employment, income and livelihood for a majority of poor—is their basic asset and grabbing it has become an easy mode of business expansion for the corporate world with the backing of the state.

Kalyan Sanyal[3] observes that the post-colonial capitalist development is an unprecedented experience. The direct producers are alienated from their means of production leaving nothing to fall back on for their livelihood except their labour power. This is done for accumulation of capital. He maintains that this capital constantly seeks to increase the rate of exploitation by changing the organic composition of capital that results in fall in employment. This is also done by depressing work opportunities to all those alienated from assets. He lamented that such displaced labour are fated to a world of excluded, redundant and the dispensable and in turn creates a vast *waste land* inhabited by people whose lives as producers have been subverted and destroyed by the thrust of the process of expansion of capital. It is also important to note that such people never get an opportunity to work in this world of capital. Thus the post-colonial capital works for its own self-expansion constantly and produces *surplus labour*.

Sanyal argues that the surplus population thus produced are not the casualties of capitalists accumulation but of the *arising of capital*. He maintains that this *surplus labour* is engendered on the basis of regular contraction of ***necessary labour*** (labour required for capital's own reproduction). This capital is engaged which increases the rate of exploitation and reduces the necessary labour and results in redundancy of labour power—the waste land—whose existence he observes is permanent outside the capital.

Sanyal's concept of *decapitalization* (non-capitalist production) explains transfer of a part of the surplus produced in the capitalist sector (that is meant for formation of new capital) to the non-capitalist or to set a need-based economy in which the dispossessed are rehabilitated in non-capitalist production activities. He argues that the capital's *"being is never completed.*[4] *He made it clear that the inscription of the waste land is a perpetual state of becoming*. He further observes that the forms of employment provided by the *need-based* economy are: self-employment, household employment with family labour or different forms of collective/communal organizations of production and explains that the household as one of the *waste-land* that is excluded and not given the option to work for capital. This produces surplus value for capital in the form of continuous reproduction of labour power.

Bryceson (1999)[5] states that SAP is a mechanism that entails rising input costs and poor market prospects for peasants by dispossession of their land assets for capital accumulation. These changes are combined with the rising cash needs of households' reproduction due to imposition of 'user charges' at health centres, schools and rising food prices. All such factors led to intensified households' diversification strategies and proliferation of income earners within the rural households.

Alpa and Barbara Harris (2011)[6] maintain that in the last thirty years the structure of agrarian property has clearly been transformed and the structure of land holdings become **pear-shaped** with 63 per cent of its producers owning holdings of less than one hectare. Citing the NSSO (2003) data they analyse that only a little over five per cent of producers own more than three hectares and just 0.52 per cent own more than 10 hectares.

It is further observed that some of the social categories that were not landlords earlier have become dominant farmers.

They stated that the sharecropping tenancy that constituted 6.5 per cent of operated area has been replaced and became different from old ones. They found that people are losing interest in village affairs and landlordship as the basis of social status and political power diminished.

They observed that the female labour that is displaced from land (for capital accumulation) has **not entered the industrial sector.** They cited NSSO data (2004-05) to confirm that the non-farm rural economy accounted for $1/5^{th}$ of total employment and concluded saying that the largest number of new jobs increased in the category of self-employment where they control means of production for exchange and **exploit their own labour**. These production activities are reproduced through family relationships. The author suggests distributive land reforms and multiple livelihood options for reproduction of rural households.

Vaidyanathan's (2010)[7] study based on 232 districts in the country observes that in the mid 60s a little over 71 per cent of the geographical area was available for cultivation. By the 1990s the geographical area being the same, the gross cropped area has increased by 15 per cent while the net sown area increased barely three per cent. He argues that in the low rain-fed area the available land for cultivation and the incidence of cultivable waste and pastures relative to available land is highest compared to irrigated area. He adds that the estimated areas of irrigation both in the ground water sources and of surface systems increased manifold during this period. However, it is noted that in industrialized areas the situation is different.

Vaidyanathan identified relatively low land-man ratio, unequal distribution of land ownership, a high degree of subdivision and fragmentation of holdings, predominance of small farms operated mostly by owner cultivators, the limited role of tenancy and high dependency on wage labour for agricultural operations as distinguishing characteristics of Indian agriculture. He maintains that the wage labour plays a significant role in Indian agriculture and argues that according to the 2001 Census nearly 40 per cent of workers engaged in agriculture were wage labourers. There are very few purely wage labour-dependent farmers or wholly family labour-dependent farms. The relative importance of the two sources of labour is function of holding size, caste composition of the population and of land owners. Incidence of wage labour tends to be higher in regions with a relatively high proportion of SCs which have traditionally been excluded from land ownership.

The above studies have shown the nature of liberalized policy in case of land displacing the labour for its capital accumulation. The displaced labour do not find a place in industries. Their compensation money enters into unproductive circulation. They produce for market exchange by exploiting their own labour. Most of these studies (except Apha and Barbara Harris) are not long duration observations. These macro studies cannot show the gradual processes involved in the displacement of households and the process of dispossession of land. The present study fills this gap by presenting the different stages of marginalization and displacement and their implications to female labour.

The following studies show the relation between the dispossession of land and implications for female labour.

Shahra Razavi (2003).[8] This study observes that the land rights to women is a central concern of today and further observes women's centrality to diversify livelihood, their interest in land as in male dominated households and as members of vulnerable social classes, and community that face risk of land alienation and entitlement failure in the context of liberalization are more politicized and contested. He argues that the unequal land rights contributed to female poverty, subordination, sustenance and reproduction.

Deniz Kandiyoti (2003)[9] in her account of post-socialist agricultural reforms and livelihoods crisis in Uzbekistan argues that the programmes of stabilization were deflationary. Non-agricultural female employment suffered recession. Many industries were closed or operated with reduced workforce that receives irregular wages or payments in kind. The restructuring of collective farming enterprises have gone for progressive retrenchment of labour that disproportionately affected women. These retrenched female labour crowded into casual agricultural workforce and taken up precarious forms of self-employment in informal trade and services.

Utsa Patnaik[10] (2003) in her insightful study traces the present-day rural crisis to one; the decelerating neoliberal policies that have political support; two, the removal of all barriers to free movement of financial capital; three, piling up the stocks. These problems compelled the peasants for shifts in cropping patterns from food production to export-driven production. This shift in food crops along with cut in investments in agriculture she maintains had affected negatively on per capita food availability.

She points out that the cuts in the state's development expenditures in post-1991, caused the collapse of rural non-farm employment, rural wages and consequent decline in mass incomes. She held that this led to a magnitude of crisis that is unprecedented since the great depression 70 years ago. She concludes that the dominance of financial capital being the main reason for today's crisis as was the case in 1920.

Bina Agarwal (2003)[11] argues that absorption of women and men into the non-agricultural sector has slowed down since 1987-88 and especially since 1991. She observed that for women the compound growth rate of non-agricultural employment fell from 5.2 per cent over 1978-88 to 0.2 per cent in 1988-94. She points out very sharply the differences in absorption of additional workforce male and female where the absorption of male labour force in non-agriculture was 14 per cent while it has been less than one per cent of female labour force addition. She maintains that this caused a marked gender difference in non-farm employment and this low absorption of female workforce led them either to get crowded in agriculture or take on precarious forms of work in the informal sector. She noted that 58 per cent of all male workers, 78 per cent of all female workers and 86 per cent of all rural female workers are in agriculture. This dependency for women on agriculture declined by less than four per cent since 1972-3. From this she concludes that land is central for rural female employment. The collective investments and cultivation by women helps them in availing of subsidized leased/purchase land. She suggests that the main sources of arable land for this collective cultivation can be acquired from state, family and market which could go as a new way of land reforms.

She cites to support her argument a detailed survey done by Chadha on three states AP, Bihar and UP (in 1992) which shows that in terms of daily household earnings from self-employment in rural off-farm sector in all three states small farmers' households earned substantially more than landless labour households. His emphasis on AP shows that farmers' earnings from this source were eight times more than those of landless households. Based on this evidence, Bina Agarwal argues that even for ensuring rural women's entry into higher earning segments of non-farm, an initial strengthening of land rights is essential.

Both the studies of Bina Agarwal (2003) (in case of India) and Kandiyoti (2003) (in case of rural Uzbekistan) show that women tend to be largely concentrated in the low-and insecure-earnings at the end of the non-farm occupational spectrum. The authors argue that marginalization of women's land rights can be detrimental to the development and consolidation of agrarian reform settlements.

M.S. Swaminathan and Kanayo F. Nwanze[12] stated that two billion people worldwide depend on small farms for food and livelihood. Small farmers produce 41% of the country's food grains that contribute to the food security. They maintain that women make up a large percentage of small farmers in the developing world. Small farmers generate 30-60 per cent of GDP, 60 per cent of employment and 80 per cent of the farm land in part of Asia. He suggested that women should be given attention in training in bio-gas technology, solar energy technology, technology in millets production which grows in dry lands. He adds that they should be trained to make millet malt to enhance nutrients and income and to be trained to improve moisture levels in the land and land entitlements.

Govind Kelkar (2011)[13] argues that female labour is discriminated in ownership of assets and in education against their livelihood security and autonomy and against the enhancement of their capabilities. She maintains that her access to opportunity to enhance capabilities in terms of learning technology, raising credit and exercising the control over other productive resources, participating in capability enhancing government programmes are limited. The public policy has been silent on these factors. Calling for policy attention to address these persistent gender discriminations that mark lack of endowments at the starting point to women in ownership and control of productive assets.

P.V. Satish and Pimbert (1999)[14] studied Medak district (under study) and have shown that more than two million people living in 12 hundred villages in the district are with fallow holdings that account for at least 50 per cent of land. This trend is a clear base for dispossession of land.

A study by scientists[15] who wanted to promote the biodiversity in the district Medak stated that they found a great difference in choices of crops by men and women in agriculture in the district. Women wanted food crops to be produced while men wanted commercial crops.

The above studies brought out the importance of small and marginal farmers in terms of contribution to production and employment. Because of development of adverse conditions the farmers kept their holdings fallow. The suggestions were made by the scholars for imparting skills to the displaced female labour in the non-farm employment. The studies explain that female labour start at a low level of production and there is silence on the part of the state in expanding capabilities to them. The present study however is different from these studies in the way of data collection from the field. This study presents time series data collected from the same farm households from 1979 to 2010. This study unlike many other studies has divided and examined the labour of the village engaged in agriculture, finance and production industry. The study probed into employment of female labour in both farm and non-farm sectors. The analyses are carried out across intra and interrelated sectarian research of these areas. This gives changes in employment and impacts and reason for the change. The study also probes into the social 'structure' emerging in the light of agrarian transition and changing employment of female labour. The studies suggest policy interventions for this broad spectrum of intra and inter-related issues of female labour. In the backdrop of the analysis and conclusions of the above studies the following data on three surveys on the village under study is framed for insightful analysis.

Three surveys: Emerging Trends. *Both the studies of Bina Agarwal (2003) (in case of India) and Kandiyoti (2003) (in case of rural Uzbekistan)* show that women tend to be largely concentrated in the low-and insecure-earnings at the end of the non-farm occupational spectrum. The author argues that marginalization of women's land rights can be detrimental to the development and consolidation of agrarian reform settlements.

The three consecutive surveys of the present work bring out the changes in farm land and female employment on farm and non-farm from 1979 to 2009-10.

The first survey shows 82 per cent of the village households were engaged in agriculture with 62 per cent of female labour of the village. More than 90 per cent of arable land was under cultivation. Agricultural resources and infrastructures were supported by the state. Commercialization of paddy cultivation with GR package was increasing the incomes of the cultivators. The paddy cultivation was female intensive and wages were paid in kind up to the late 1970s. Therefore the female labour from small and marginal cultivators' households prioritized paddy cultivation work for their subsistence incomes. This gets in the composition of male and female hired agricultural labour in the village. The male hired labour constitutes a mere 10.75 per cent and from female it was as high as 75 per cent from their respective working population in 1979. It is very significant to note that the family and hired labour composition has changed in the thirty years across the social groups. The following social composition existed during 1979.

The female hired labour worked in association with caste and class hierarchy. Seventy-two per cent of the forward castes work on their own fields, while only 28 per cent of them accept hired work. From the backward castes 24 per cent work on their own lands and 76 per cent accept hired work. From scheduled castes a mere 13 per cent work on own land and 87 per cent work as hired labour. This well-performing agriculture provided stable and intensive paid work to women.

The second survey (during 1995-96) shows after the 1990s the priority for agriculture and for development of public sector undertakings were undermined by shifting policy objectives. With no development support for agriculture and no regulations of market processes, the input prices started rising. Many of the small and marginal cultivators shifted to non-farm activities although, however a small number still struggled to sustain themselves in cultivation on account of lack of (proper) alternative livelihoods. The high growth of industrial development in the region did not provide new employment particularly to women of old generation. The industrial employment and incomes by this time were made insecure by the new industrial policy. On the side of social change fifty-eight per cent of the joint families turned into unit families. Although 1,333 acres out of 1,450.41 acres of geographical area of the village was under cultivation, the land sales were picking up compared to the period of the first survey.

The number of cultivator households shrank from 82 per cent in 1979 to 38 per cent by the second survey in 1995-96 in the total households of the village. The percentage of female cultivators among the social groups SCs, BCs and FCs were constituted 13, 1.4 and about 40 per cent in 1979 and by 1989 got reduced to 'nil' among SCs, 4 per cent among BCs and 22 per cent among FCs. This in-turn changed to one per cent, 14 per cent and 18 per cent by 1999 respectively out of the total workers of their respective social category. On the whole the composition of the female labour constituted 13 per cent on hired labour and three per cent on own land out of the total female workers. The female workers on own farm land across the social categories constituted one per cent, four and three per cent from SC, BC, and from FCs respectively. In the hired workers category they constituted 21, 18 and 1.6 per cent of the total female hired workers in that order (Vanamla, 2003 report). This shows there is decrease in overall cultivation. This loss of cultivable land resulted in the number of forced housewives which rose as high as 59 per cent of total female workers during 1995-96. This housewifization is observed against the achievement of educational levels that are above state average (*Statistical Handbook*, Sanga Reddy). This increase in housewives reveals that once a woman shifts from land as alternative employment is not available.

The third survey shows that the small and marginal farmers were forced to sell their holdings which became uneconomical due to rising input prices. The rise in input prices far exceeded rise in output prices. The cultivators incurred a loss of Rs 10,000 on every acre cultivated. The extensive sales led to land scarcity that needed to make their small holding viable for cultivation (due to the price bubble, and SEZ policy). As most of the land holdings owned is small and uneconomical, that led to further sale of arable land. By 2009-10 the land under cultivation shrank to a mere 237.055 acres. It is significant that an area of 604 acres, which works out to 82 per cent of farm land has moved out of cultivation in the decade of the later 2000s. This made many landed households turn into irregular cultivators of alternative holdings by 2009-10 (keeping parts of land fallow). The marginal and small cultivators that own land quite often worked as labour in the precarious job market keeping land fallow. With these changes in cultivation only 15 per cent of households have sown in the year of the last survey of this study (see Table 7, Vanamala sample survey, Annexure 4). This drastic reduction in the households under cultivation became a fraction of the village. Several economic, social and policy factors acted and counteracted for shift of huge farm land to non-farm. This has led to different social economic consequences.

The shift of farm land occurred in a dual way and in two phases from small marginal and from wage-dependent farmers. The acquisition of land for industries and corporations inspired the shift to real estate and speculative business. This is the first phase. The second phase of land shift occurred on account of unviable holding size and unviable expenses on cultivation. This happened due to shift of farm land to cultivable waste or to fallows that has increased to a significant proportion of 35 per cent of farm land by 2009-10. The shift of land that has been under labour intensive paddy/food crop was to that of no-female-labour-taking-non-food/orchids by the wage-dependent cultivators. Still the other way of shift of land happened on account of shift of cultivation from the village. There are also trends of concentration of land that adopted capital intensive and labour displacing cultivation. These shifts of land from farm had severely reduced the holding to a size that is unviable for cultivation. Such holdings increased to constitute 83 per cent of land owners. The size of holding under cultivation is the function of female employment. The intensity in compression of holding size and its magnitude is evident from the empirical data.

The Processes of Compression in Holding Size: As has been already stated the shift of land was in a dual way. The small and marginal farmers pushed it (sold) to non-farm activities while the wage-dependent cultivators have consolidated it for commercial crops. The data on movement of both dry and wet land shows that it followed the dual pattern. The shift of dry land caused a fall in holding size between the years 1995-96 and 2009-10. This is clear from the size of land slab of less than one acre did not exist during 1995-96. By 2009-10 about 10 per cent of total dry land fell into this land slab (See Tables 4, 5, 6 & 6a). Sventy per cent of dry land was in the distribution in the subsequent upper slab of 1-2.5 acres. It also fell to 43 per cent by 2009-10. This makes it clear that the small and marginal farmers were selling the land to non-farm. With this the land size of this section was shrinking to a size that turned into unviable further for cultivation and for further dispossession. These unviable holdings resulted in a drastic shift either to fallows or to land market resulting in shift of female labour to non-farm occupations. This shift of farm land shifted female labour to non-farm. This in turn created acute shortage of female agricultural labour for wage-dependent cultivators.

The acute shortage of female agricultural labour resulted in consolidation and shift of farm land by the wage-dependent cultivators to shift from labour intensive food crops to low labour intensive orchids and to other low labour intensive crops. The consolidation and commercialization of farm land got concentrated. The following data shows it.

The dry land slab of 2.6 to 5 acres was 16 per cent in 1995-96 (Table 4). It increased to more than 26 per cent by 2009-10 (Table 5). The area in the subsequent slab of 5.1 to 10 acres acres also has increased from about seven per cent to 21 per cent that works out to three times of its area existed in 1995-96 (Table 4 & 5). These processes explain the upward mobility of land and towards concentration. Perhaps these are the families that turned into family farms.

The data on the land slabs of 10.1 to 20 acres, and 20 and above acres shows that more than 13 per cent of the cultivators shifted their cultivation to outside the village. This resulted in decrease in farm land that is available for hired labour and for sharecropper tenant cultivators. This is because of acute shortage of agricultural wage labour. The data on mobility of wet land shows that about 22 acres or 19.17 per cent of wet land area under cultivation was owned by about 67 per cent of households in the land slab of less than one acre in 2009-10. There were no holdings in the slab of less than one acre in 1995-96 (Table 6a). About 95 per cent and 98 per cent of wet land-holdings of irrigated type I & type II were in distribution of the slab of 1-2.5 acres. The area from this land-slab fell drastically to about 54 per cent of total irrigated land existed in 2009-10. The land slab of 2.6-5 acres has gone up from 13

(Table 6 & 6a) acres during 1995-96 to almost double constituting about 18 acres. This explains clearly that the wet land shifted from lower level marginal farmers (1-2.5 acres) to upper level marginal farmers (2.6-5 acres) holders. The land slab of 10-20 acres, acquired more than 16 acres of irrigated land (13 per cent) by a single household which this type of distribution never existed in the history of the village. The earlier land distribution shows that even the rich farmers did not have a higher area of irrigated land. This explains that even the wet land that produces staple food- rice- for family consumption and provides food security to the family was moving away from marginal farmers to the higher land slabs.

The above shift of both dry and wet land reduced the land holding size of small and marginal farmers resulting in unaffordable conditions to invest in rising costs of inputs. From this evidence it is argued that the small and marginal farmers sustained themselves in cultivation during the last 30 years as they had higher land holding size (may be because of land reforms) together with the support from the state for development of irrigation, infrastructure and input subsidies and regulated levy operations and stability and support of minimum support price for paddy. They also had support of incomes earned by family members with the employment in public sector industries around the village. This agriculture was a sought-after livelihood for the landless hired labour households till the late 1980s. From the late 1990s the rising input costs pushed agriculture into a crisis. An experienced cultivator who was selected as 'Adarsha Rythu' in the village has presented an account of the crisis in the market madiated agriculture of small and marginal farmers as follows.

He observed that the peasant cannot sustain himself in paddy cultivation "as inputs prices swallow the additional value of labour." He mentions an increase in input prices over the previous year. The increase on DAP was by Rs 75 per kg, on urea by Rs 75 per kg, on pesticides by Rs 120 (from Rs 60 per kg), on chlorides Rs 80 per kg, on seeds by Rs 125 (from Rs 400). During this time the rent of the tractor increased by three times costing Rs 100 per hour. The male labour charges have gone up by 50% costing Rs 190 per person per day. He observed that these costs have gone up to almost 200 per cent forcing the land sales. "The land sales were triggered with the land boom bubble created during this decade. The land prices rose from Rs 40,000 to Rs 80,0000/ per acre that tempted the farmers for sale of land. Even for this rate, he stated, land is not available because of the speculative business of real estate. The land sales reached its peak sales in this decade reducing the farm land to 349 acres. The 'Adarsha Ritu' says that government is competing in the land market with the peasants". The government instead of being supportive to farmers by improving irrigation facilities it has enacted mindless policies. He cited the policy of free imports of food products and said, "When farmers are cultivating paddy, why should Government import rice from Karnataka, Maharashtra and Chandighar"? This policy is making our paddy market flooded with paddy and facilitates millers to buy their paddy at throw-away prices. He maintained that "the peasants in this region are weak and unless they sell their produce they cannot reinvest in the next crop". He added that "banks do not lend" to farmers. These factors together forced the land sales.

Impact on Female Labour: Land holding size is a decisive factor for female employment on land. This dispossession of land displaced the female labour from land. The reduction in the size of the arable holdings changed the per-capita land holding size from 4.5 acres in 1995-96 to 0.6389 in 2009-10 (Vanamala, 2003) resulting in reduction of female agricultural labour from 70 per cent in the 1970s to 17.5 per cent in 2009-10 (fourteen female workers out of a sample of 80 stated that their main occupation is agricultural labour (Vanamala sample data collected in 2009-10). The percentage of female agricultural labour across the social categories has been on the downward spiral. The most affected category was the SCs who depended more on hired labour. The female labour ratio was 81:47:18-from SCs, BCs and FCs respectively during 1979 that has changed to 71: 56:12 (per cent in the total respective social group workers) by 1989. It further reduced to 21:18:1.6 by 1999.

This hired labour in agriculture is hit very hard by a new policy that came into existence as part of flexible labour policy. The "flexible, mobile labour group working under a contractor" has cornered the village female agricultural work with the support of the village wage-dependent cultivators. The village labour had no alternative but to shift from farm to non-farm work[16]. This resulted in adverse consequences for both female labour and wage-dependent cultivators. The female labour could not find any productive, decent livelihood activity in non-farm and the wage-dependent cultivators were forced to shift from food to non-food crop by 2009-10.

Processes of Mobile Female Labor Groups: The flexible mobile female agricultural labour groups under a contractor moved into the village from outside with the enactment of the new policy in the 1990s. This mobile labour institution played a very critical role in displacement of village agricultural female labour from farm work. It was also responsible for shifting the wage payments from kind to total monetary form. The landed wage labour dependents preferred mobile labour over village labour as they can pay wages only in money and to overcome other age-old practices that were institutionalized in cultivation work. This preference of landed led to a hostile relationship with village hired labour.

To counter this act of preference of wage-dependent landed for mobile groups, village hired labour formed into a group like their counterparts under the contract system without a contractor and demanded work from wage labour dependent cultivators. While with great difficulty they could contract some land to work on. The wages paid to them for the work they managed to get was very low. The amount as shared among the village groups, worked out was Rs 6 (six) per head for the four hours work they got. They learnt that it was a "distress employment". These women have withdrawn from this work to become housewives.

The hard hit female hired village labour that constituted more than 70 per cent of the working age group in the 1970s decreased to 13 per cent by 1995-96 (Vanamala, 2003). However the mobile female labour groups moved away from the village to other places when the overall agricultural activity got reduced in the village. This shift of mobile labour changed labour relations from that of surplus labour to acute shortage of agricultural female labour in the village. It is very important to observe the changes in wages in the context of scarcity. The scarcity of female labour for cultivation improved their bargaining power to bargain for the payment of wages in kind (paddy) from those cultivators that adopted manual labour more. However it is very striking that such massive shortage in female agricultural labour has not influenced the changes either in the wage structure of female labour or in the wage relation between male and female. The increase in wages over the period was marginal. This is clear from the rigidity in increase in the wages of female labour.

The following data shows a marginal increase in wages.

Table 9: Agricultural Wages Under Mechanized Cultivation[17] in 2009-10

Agricultural Wages in Rs				*Wages as per Labour Act in Rs*			
Season		*Off Season*		*Season*		*Off Season*	
Male	*Female*	*Male*	*Female*	*Male*	*Female*	*Male*	*Female*
250	190	150	120	100	-	90	-

Collected from field in 2009-10. The female agricultural wages increased from Rs 30 in the 1970s to Rs 190 (in season) in 2009-1, that increase has not attracted any additional labour into agricultural work.

A series of strategic policy enactments by the state and the consequent social changes have caused a crisis in the labour relations. The strategic policy promulgations and their impact on land and labour relations show the following trend.

Changes in Land, Labour and Community Relations: The abolition of the office of Patwari in the 1980s and shift of this power into the formal village office has changed land and labour relations in the village. The power base of Patwari, who was OC, was control over the entire village land. The loss of control over village land dissolved the power centre. The state enacted policies like the 73rd amendment created a political space for BCs. For the first time in the history of the village the BCs entered the formal political power with reservation of the post of the Sarpanch. This shift of political power from OC which they enjoyed for more than 25 years, reduced the political power of this section. The series of policies that were contributed for the erosion of the power of OC (power centre) can be mentioned as the New Economic Policy in 1990, the policy on Self-Help Groups and Act on MGNREG and ordinance on direct crop loans to tenants. Thus, the control over land, the control over political power and control over economic activity together reduced the power of OCs. The historical institutions that played a positive role in protection of land and labour relations disappeared.

The traditional, informal land committees structured by the landed communities for protection of their land from transfer to other communities disappeared. The interviews with people indicate that the BC Munnuru Kapu community which constitutes the majority in the total population was mainly a farming community with very small land holdings. This community maintained land committees till the 1980s. Thus the land committees acting as informal legal institutions against transfer, disappeared. Thus the land and labour relations got disturbed.

Another community among the BCs (Kurma) that enjoyed full employment of both male and female of the household based on farm land. The Kurma, shepherd community was most powerful in economic conditions followed by informal power (political and cultural) in the village up to the late 1980s. This relation of employment on land got upset with the introduction of the new chemical fertilizer technology package in agriculture and commercialization of food crops. They lost their chain of male and female shepherd-based well-performing occupations. They turned from a powerful voice in the village to voiceless precarious labour. There is a very interesting turning for this community with the introduction of the 73rd amendment bill. With enactment of this bill, the Sarpanch position went as a reserved post to a BC candidate. With this change this community in the recent years mobilized the people of their caste to regain their strength in politics. They organized new political community-based institutions. The forms of events in this community are observed as the 'Mallanna jathera'. The land and labour relations were disrupted with division of the joint family system. The data on division of joint family shows that 58 per cent of the joint families changed into nuclear families by 2009-10 (Vanamala, 2003). This resulted in the further fragmentation of 82 per cent of patta land (legally registered). This disruption of joint families followed in massive land disputes that also resulted in suicides in some cases in the village. The land sales processes are observed as follows.

The officials and public representative (Sarpanch) and real speculators of land had nexuses in land sales. The Gram Panchayat officer is authorized by the state ordinance to be the protector of land against any illegal transactions of land ownership. This officer is expected legally to permit the seller of land to transfer the land ownership to buyers. The nexus among powers with fake gimmicks resulted in friction in inter-personal relations of landed family members and between families and official, non-official power and people. These strained relations between people and officials affected the official benefits like distribution of ration-cards, health cards, old age and disability pension cards, tax fixation on house property, etc.

The land and labour relations were further disrupted with the strategic decisions of the state. With the strategic idea to favor the capital the MGNREGP labour has been illigally used by the corporate contractor. This resulted in scarcity (demand) of labour for agricultural work and also resulted in raising the agricultural wages, as paddy cannot be grown without wage labour. This act of shift of agricultural labour to corporate work shows a disadvantage not only to the paddy cultivators but equally harmful to the labour. As the MGNREGP labour would be thrown out once the contractor completes his project. The same labour when they are back to the village finds no land is left to do farm work. The data shows that both the small and marginal farmers and also the wage-dependent cultivators regularly changed the crop pattern. They introduced cost-saving methods in their cultivation either by shifting from paddy crop to dry crops (by small and marginal farmers), or by shifting from paddy crop to non-food and non-labour intensive commercial crops (by wage-dependent cultivators). Thus the forced commercialization and shift from food crops would cause a serious problem for female agricultural labour that return to village employment in the near future. Such disruptions in the land and labour relations, the female labour cannot find a decent livelihood in the village. Following these changes in agricultural employment the next chapter traces the changes in opportunities in non-farm employment for male and female labour. The track of employment, income and quality of work for males and females within the traditional agrarian non-farm sector followed by the modern non-farm employment and its quality of work life for those displaced female labour from land.

REFERENCES

1. Michael Levien (2011), Special Economic Zones and Accumulation by Dispossession in India, Blackwell Publishers and also see *Journal of Agrarian Change,* Vol. 11, No. 4 October 2011, pp. 454-483.
2. Sundaresan (2011), International Conference on Applied Economics "Special Economic Zone and Accumulation by Dispossession," Blackwell Publishers.
3. Kalyan Sanyal, *Rethinking Capitalist Development: Primitive Accumulation, Governmentality and Post-Colonialism,* Routledge, Taylor & Francis Group, London, New York, New Delhi, 2007.
4. It is important to note Kalyan Sanyal's concept of need economy that a peasant engaged in cash crop production to earn a certain required level of income, belongs to the need economy. He justifies this based on the huge informal sector described as the petty commodity production in the third world.
5. Shahra Razavi (2003), Introduction: An Agrarian Change, Gender and Land Rights, *Journal of Agrarian Change*, Vol. 3, Nos. 1&2 January and April, pp. 2-32.

6. NSSO 2003-04 and also see Alpa and Barbara Harris White (2011) Resurrecting Scholarship on Agrarian Transformation, *Economic & Political Weeky*, Vol. Xl, Vol. No. 39.
7. Vaidyanathan (2010), *Agricultural Growth in India: Role of Technology, Incentives and Institutions*, Oxford University Press.
8. Shara Razvi (2003), Introduction: An Agrarian Change,Gender and Land Rights, *Journal of Agrarian Change*, Vol. 3, Nos. 1&2 January and April, pp. 2-32.
9. Shahra Razavi (2003), op. cit. (Introduction: An Agrarian Change, Gender and Land Rights, *Journal of Agrarian Change*, Vol. 3, Nos. 1&2 January and April, p. 2-32).
10. Bina Agarwal (1998), Disinherited Peasants-Disadvantaged Workers: A Gender Perspective on Land and Livelihood *Economic & Political Weekly*, Vol. 33, No. 13, March 26-April 26.
11. *Hindu* Editorial, November 14, 2011.
12. Govind Kelkar Gender and Productive Assets: Implications for Women's Economic Security and Productivity, *Economic & Political Weekly*, June 4, 2011. In India the inheritance laws governing Hindus were reformed through the Hindu Succession Amendment Act 2005 to inherit agricultural land by women. In practice this law is not upheld by private and public enforcement or changed customs and traditions favouring inclusion of women not only for ownership but also in management of productive assets as a right. Part IV, para 2 of Article 15 and 16 of CEDAW states that all signatory states must "recognize women's rights to own, inherit and administer (control right) property in their own names; provide equal rights for both spouses in respect of ownership, acquisition, management, administration" (UN 1980). The WB's rural strategy (2003) suggests that improvement in the well-being of the poor will only be possible through enhancement of their productive, social and environmental assets. (WB 2003, 40).
13. P.V. Satish and Pimbert (1999) Reclaiming Diversity, Restoring Livelihoods in Medak District: A Study by Dekkan Development Centre, Internet.
14. SANET_MG – on Poor Women Farmers: Report of Rheagala, in Medak District (2006): Internet.
15. A majority of the paddy cultivators had come to depend on mechanization. Out of the total cultivator households a mere 5-10 households depend on traditional bullock power. This cultivation system uses the bullock ploughing system. The payment of wages are both in kind and cash. The per acre charges are six bags of paddy and Rs 5000 cash. With the manual harvesting system the grass (animal feed) is safe. In machine harvesting it is damaged.

3

Strategies for Sustenance: Farm and Non-Farm Activities

The analysis on the three surveys in previous chapter shows a significant reduction in the area under cultivation and a consequential reduction in the size of farm holding resulting in unviable for cultivation. These changes in farming paved the way for female cultivations or "feminized cultivation".

However on account of high costs of production farming yielded low value added. Therefore, this marginalised cultivation was done with increased unpaid female labour. This marginalized farming resulted in innovative strategies through communitarian and co-operative practices to reduce the costs on cultivation without any improvement in the status of these female cultivatiors, the drudgery went up both at domestic and farm side.

The following innovations that women cultivators practised on their farming are some of the instances for showing their increased drudgery.

Cost saving by changing the crops: The data presented in table (10) shows the changes brought by the cultivators in the choice of crops to reduce the cost of production between 1995-96 and 2009-10.

The data in Table (11) shows that the land allotted for paddy, the major food crop of the region (second highest labour intensive) was 41.97 per cent of the area sown. The tomato crop (first highest female labour intensive) was placed in the second

Table 10: Crop-wise Land Sown by Sample Cultivators in 1995-96

Crop	*Crop-wise area allotted (in acres)* 1	*Yield per acre (in quintals)* 2	*Price (per quintal)* 3	*Value per acre (in Rs)* = 2X3
Paddy	95.24 (41.97)	25	700	17,500
Tomato	55.10 (24.28)	30	400	12,000
Onion	16.28 (7.17)	60	500	30,000
Ground nut	20.21(8.90)	11	1100	12,100
Sorghum	23.05 (10.15)	11	700	7,700
Chilly	3.3 (1.49)	06	2000	12000
Wheat	01.00 (0.44)	7.5	600	4500
Curdi	07.39 (3.25)	03	1500	4500
Redgram	05.25 (2.31)	08	600	4800
Total	226.90 (!00.00)	-	-	-

Collected from respondents in the village in 1995-96.

highest place with an allotment of 24.28 per cent of land. Sorghum occupied third place with 10.15 per cent of land allocation, ground nuts and onions occupied fourth and fifth places with 8.90 per cent and 7.17 per cent of land allocations out of the total area sown. When conditions in cultivation worsened for paddy, the cultivators opted for other crops. The following data shows that in the year 2009-10 some of these crops were substituted for paddy.

From Table (11) it is clear that although the area allocated for paddy is highest among the crops sown, however the percentage of allocation for it has come down from 41.97 per cent in 1995-96 (Table 10) to about 39 per cent of total cultivated area in 2009-10 (Table 11). This decrease in land allotted for paddy has taken place despite the increase in yield per acre, price per quintal and increase in the gross value per acre (from Rs 17,500 to Rs 37,200) at present prices. These dynamics in paddy cultivation account for cultivation of paddy being substituted with other crops to circumvent the problems of paddy cultivation.

Table 11: Change in the Area Allocation for Crops by Sample households (in acres) in 2009-10

Crop	*Area in %Acres*	*Yield per Acre*	*Price Per. Q.*	*Value per Acre (Rs)*	*Value per acre at (95-96) prices*
Paddy	120.00 (38.83)	40	900	36,000	40x700= 28,000
Sorghum	40.00 (12.94)	11	1600	17,600	11x700=7,700
Tomato	30.00 (9.70)	25	750	18,750	25x400=10,000.
Cotton	13.00 (4.20)	11	3500	38,500	11x no cotton in 95
Maize	14.00 (4.53)	20	800	16,000	20x no maize in 95
Horticulture	92.00 (29.77)	-	-	-	No yield
Total	309.00				——

Source: Collected from Gram Panchayat records

The land allotted to the paddy crop (table 11) has come down despite increase in the value of produce. In real terms the value per acre of paddy worked out to Rs 28,000 in 2009-10 which was higher than the value earned in 1995-96 per acre (see Table 8 Rs 17,500 per acre).

The tomato crop occupies first rank in labour intensity. The area allotted to the tomato crop in 2009-10 was 1/3 of this area allotted to this crop in 1995-96. This area shrank despite increase in output price per quintal of tomato to almost double from Rs 400 to Rs 750 during this period. This decrease in land allotted to the tomato crop could be explained in terms of the labour shortage and consequent fall in area.Therefore the land allotted for the paddy and tomato have been been shrinking (Table 11).

The third highest allocation of area is for sorghum both during 1995-96 and in 2009-10. However it is important to note that the area allocated has been almost double from 23 acres to 40 acres during these years. It is a second staple food of the subsistence farmers. The increase in the cropped area under sorghum can be explained that it is non labour intensive. Therefore it appears to escape from the high cost on labour inputs in the paddy cultivation. Sorghum has been substituted.

A significant substitution for the above crops seems to be commercial horticulture. A section of the cultivators (wage labour dependent) were forced to select non-labour intensive crops like maze and cotton 30 per cent of land has gone into it in the place of labour intensive crops like paddy and tomato to escape from labour problems.

The traditional paddy food crop has been substituted by other non-food commercial crops. More than four per cent of land is allotted for each of the newly diversified commercial crops like cotton and maize. Out of the total cropped area 30 per cent of the land was diverted to commercial crops. From the remaining 60 per cent cropped area, 30 per cent of it was used to grow HYV- 1010 variety mono-crop commercial paddy (which is not useful for staple food) for earning cash incomes this crop is grown. This has been dominating at present among the paddy varieties grown for the market. This crop is preferred by cultivators as it is heavier than the traditional varieties. The respondents stated that 70 kgs of 1010 variety is equivalent to 100 kgs of traditional Sonamasoori variety. This is purchased by the food processing market which is linked with the business centre in Mumbai (the village is located on the National Highway connecting Mumbai). This helped the farmers in recovery of loss of income from traditional paddy which was high in input cost.

Maize is another low labour intensive commercial crop in the area that was started after the poultry farms were set up in the region. Poultry farms buy maize directly from the farmers and relieve them from the problems of millers. The other cost reduction methods were also adopted.

Cost Saving on Machine: The rents of tractors are unaffordable.[1] The lower the land holding size, the higher dependence on capital intensive technology which works out costly. Dependence on tractors is more when a woman is cultivating. The tilling is a male task.

This explains that natural water source is a decisive factor for the paddy crop under GR technology. The bullock technology was in operation as an incentive in reduction of production costs to both the land lessee and leased under the sharecrop system. The data shows that about 74 per cent of area (table 12) under cultivation has been converted into mono crop under GR technology that required water resources (Table 12).

Table 12. Cropping System of Sample •Households in Village in 2009-10

Village Cropping System	*Land in Acres*	*Percentages*
Mono crop	257.0	73.7
Mixed crop	92.24	26.3
Total area under cultivation	349.2	100.0

Source: Collected from Gram Panchayat records.

The Annexure (6) shows 1881 acres were cultivated under natural sources during the year 1970s. This area has been reduced to less than 50 acres with destruction of natural water sources. The operation of bullock technology is possible in this small area as a measure for reduction in cost of production.

Cost Saving with Use of Female Family Labour: The paddy cultivation needs sex sequential male and female labour. These production roles are strictly **skill segregated** and "**sex sequential**". This division of labour generates more number of female work days per acre compared to man days. Apart from this division of labour the female labour involved is more physical non-machine labour than male labour (see model 1). This is because technology has not been designed to suit the tasks performed by female labour. Therefore substitution of technology for female tasks was not possible. While for the tasks performed by male labour, the substitution that reduces man days on an acre is possible. These factors worked out for more wage bill for female days than for male days despite female wages being fixed lower than men's wages. This paved the way to employ family female labour intensely to reduce the costs on paddy cultivation. The data presented in model 1 shows that the total wage bill on female activities on one acre of paddy area is Rs 18,900/and the male wage bill is Rs 8,400 (see model 1). This is a very significant factor to note in respect of female occupation. The amount/value of work done by female labour in one acre of paddy cultivation is more than the amount of work done by male labour. This prompted the cultivators to use family female labour that is readily available to save on the costs. This changed the status of female labour from hired to family. This shift of work marginalized women's occupation.

Cost Savings on Harvesting: The cultivators invented in a new method called **carpet** harvesting. From this they save an amount of Rs 1,500 on the harvesting task along with Rs 1000 that would have been incurred by them on electricity for using the harvesting machine (see model 1).

Cost Savings on Marketing: The cultivators have relocated markets for their small quantities of produce cultivated on family farms by marketing their produce from their residence instead of taking the produce to millers. This saves them transport charges of Rs 1,000. They can avoid deceitful weighing by millers.

Cost Savings by Shifting the New Tasks to Female Labour: some additional tasks are drawn-in as part of restructure of agriculture. These new tasks like marketing were rolled on to female labour. The (model 1 in this chapter), tasks done by males and females in the cultivation of paddy shows that these new tasks were done earlier by machine or males. Such tasks are shifted to female labour under cost saving strategies. With all these activities the contribution of female labour on one acre of paddy cultivation works out to not less than Rs 10,000. This forms a significant contribution of savings accounting for 1/3 of total cost of cultivation.

These newly shifted roles of female labour became regular tasks in all the paddy cultivating households. These roles are structured drawing the family and social relations into production. Despite this additional investment of time and labour by female labour, it is observed that the output value worked out to an amount lower than the value realized before restructuring.This explains the process of growing marginalization of female tasks.

The processes of marginalization of female production roles are as follows.

Marginalization of female labour on own land: The marginalization of female labour on own land of small and marginal farmers occurred in two ways; One, by sliding down to dry and low investment crops like sorgham. Such crops marginalized female labour as they are not female labour intensive. The adoption of the low investment crop- with low female labour intensity reduces their production role. Two, the marginalization of female labour occurred when the small farmers converted their holdings into family farm holdings. The female family labour employed on own farm as unpaid labour foregoes her status as worker.

Marginalization of female labour in hired work: The hired female labour was affected adversely not only with reduced area but also with the shift from food crops to other crops.

Loss of female hired work days due to change in crops: It is very interesting to observe a corollary of shortage of hired female labour and diversification of crops as a solution by the wage-dependent farmers. The shortage of female agricultural labour for wage-dependent cultivators resulted in continuous shift of land from paddy cultivation- which is female labour intensive, to a crop which is not labour intensive. This spiralled the processes of reduction in female labour.

Loss of female hired work days due to consolidation of holdings: The diversification of crops into commercial orchids involve capital-intensive technology. To facilitate the use of this capital-intensive technology the wage-dependent cultivators consolidated the holdings by entering into a **new type of joint cultivation**[3] of land of their kith and kin. The capital-intensive technology (like weeding with tractor) replaced female labour. This further reduced the work opportunities to female labour due to not only the concentration of land but due to 'labour displacing capital-intensive technology.

Loss of female hired work due to shift of cultivation to other villages: The wage labour dependent farmers have shifted their cultivation to interior villages by buying land where the agricultural labour is available and land and labour are comparatively cheaper. This further reduced the locally available farm land for cultivation. Such restructuring of cultivation by wage-dependent cultivators aggravated the problem of scarcity of land for the small and marginal farmers. These cultivators who were dependent on these landed farmers as informal tenants until the formulation of the ordinance promoting direct loars to the tenants which went against the interests of landed.

The various new strategies adopted by farmers for reduction of the production costs can be conceptualized as follows.

1. The strategies of intensification (intensive use of labour and land)
2. The strategies of substitution (use of female labour for capital).
3. The strategies of extensification (buying of additional land)
4. Strategies of diversification (shift from traditional crops to new crops).
5. Strategies of feminized and marginalized cultivation (shift of male labour tasks to female labour with no or scanty infrastructural facilities).
6. The strategies of sharing and expenditure minimizing[4] (sharing of water and land resources).
7. The strategies of pluri-activity[5] is male working in non-farm and female on farm.

Strategies for Sustenance: Non-Farm Activities

The strategies of sustenance adopted were, working in non-farm activities in the lean season for cash earnings (25%). The earnings from these activities were supplementary to (75%) farm incomes. Such interdependent, and intensive farm and non-farm together completed one production year of families. Such agrarian non-farm activities changed to modern non-agri-based non-farm activities. This part of the study presents a change in role of female labour from agri-based to non-agri based non-farm activities and their impact on female labour in 2009-10. The rural agri-based non-farm works contributed about 25 per cent of the farm incomes of the village to make agriculture a viable occupation in 1979. When cultivation started shrinking the farm land associated non-farm work also started disappearing. The non-farm work was gendered and segmented. Therefore there was no common sharing in most of these activities between males and females. While changes in land and labour relations are taking place, and no new rural female non-farm work did substitute the old and disappearing occupations. While men could enter the industries that were developed in the region. The female labour was not prepared to shift. From dignified land based work they had to go into the menial works offered by the industries. The male labour were trained in industrial skills and shifted to industry. The following analytical presentation throws light on the processes of transition in rural non-farm occupations.

The disruption of land labour relations among the Kurma Shephered community (as has already been presented earlier. This disruption swallowed of farm activities the non-farm occupation—the goats and sheep for penning crop-land—that engaged both males and females in the family. This was a highly lucrative occupation for twenty "Kurma families" that works out to 74 per cent of the families in the village penning farm land and raising wool (during 70s till early 80s), weaving blankets, while the females were engaged in spinning of the wool (during 70s till early 80s) that is used in weaving blankets. The state promoted the life-stock with subsidies under the welfare scheme. This occupation was yielding an income of Rs 96,000 per annum per family which was the highest earning among the rural non-farm occupations. This made them an influential group with a political voice in the village (Vanamala, 2003).

The rearing of sheep and goats was traditionally a male occupation. Herding for penning the farm land, cutting wool, weaving blankets and marketing are all male tasks. Women were engaged in cleaning and spinning the wool. When the chemical fertilizers package (GR technology) replaced the activity of fertilizing the land with goats and sheep the demand for these animals also fell after the 1980s. The market for these animals survived in mere transactions for consumption of animals. This shift in occupation excluded female labour from the whole process. They became unemployed housewives. The data shows that there is a high shrinkage in the animal market. During 1995-96 this animal population was 120 that got reduced to 80 by 2009-10 (Annexure 5, 6). The rural blanket market has been taken-over by the corporate woollen market. The changes forced women to become housewives. The other rural non-farm activities in the village were as follows. The sample data on **village based** (for details see Table 13) male non-farm employment during 1995-96 shows that a total of 93 males were engaged in 12 types of activities. The average income earned per head was Rs 3,145.16 per year (Vanamala, 2003, Table 8). This works out to 0.62 per cent of household gross agricultural income in 1995-96 at current prices. These incomes are cash requirements for agricultural investment and to make small and marginal holdings economically viable.

Table 13: Sample Data on Non-Farm Male Occupations and Income in the Village in 1995-96

1 *Activates*	2 *Sample number*	3 *Per head income per month*	4 *Work available in year (months)*	5 *Income in a year col. 3x4*	6 *Average hrs of work per day*	7 *Number of workers in village*	8 *Income in a year in village Col.5x7*
1. Carpenter	1	500	6	3000	8	1	3000
2. Rice mill	1	2500	4	10000	10	2	20000
3. Quarry	2	1500	12	18000	10	3	54000
4. Toddy tapper	2	1200	8	9600	10	5	48000
5. Piggery	2	100	12	1200	5	2	2400
6. Sheep & goat	2	8000	12	96000	14	20	1920000
7. Mutton business	1	2000	12	24000	8	2	48000
8. Hotel	2	1800	12	21600	14	2	43200
9. Drivers	5	1000	12	12000	14	30	360000
10. Riksha	1	40	12	4800	12	10	48000
11. Hair cutting	2	3000	12	36000	13	10	360000
12. Washing	1	300	12	3600	3	6	21600
Total	22	21940	10.5	239800	10.8	93	29,25200

(Vanamala 2003, Table 10, p. 81)

The data on female non-farm (in Table 11) works shows that there were about 18 types of works that engaged 65 female labour in the village during 1995-96. These activities were distressed, traditional; season based fleeting therefore yielded low income with long hours of work compared to male non-farm work. It is important to note that the women were engaged in pluri-activity. See the report 2003 (Vanamala) for multiple non-farm (Annexure 7) activities to get themselves engaged in work for the entire year (see Vanamala, 2003). The per head income earned in a year comes to Rs 2,72,552 (Table 11) on these activities.

Table 14: Sample Data on Female Non-Farm Occupations and Income in 1995-96

1 Activates	*2* Sample number	*3* Income Rs per month per person	*4* Work available in 9 months	*5* Income per a annum (3*4)	*6* Average hrs of work per day	*7* Total workers in village	*8* Total income of village 7x5
1. Attender	1	625	12	7,500	8	1	7,500
2. F.P. Shop	1	1,500	12	18,000	6	2	36,000
3. Supervisor	1	1,500	12	18,000	3	3	54,000
4. Rice mill	1	1,500	4	6,000	10	3	18,000
5. Vegetable business	3	1,050	12	12,600	5	3	37,800
6. Grosser	3	1,733	12	20,796	13	12	2,49,552
7. Bangle business	1	1,500	6	9,000	10	1	9,000
8. Tailoring	8	650	4	2,600	5	13	33,800
9. Snacks business	2	1,250	12	15,000	7	2	30,000
10. Quarry	2	1,500	12	18,000	10	3	54,000
11. Laundry	1	1,500	12	18,000	10	1	18,000
12. Dairy	4	2,000	12	24,000	8	4	96,000
13. L.P. making	1	1,500	2	3,000	8	4	12,000
14. Broomsticks	1	100	8	800	6	1	800
15. Mat weaving	1	200	2	400	4	6	2,400
16. Pot making	1	100	2	200	1	3	600
17. Midwife	1	100	3	300	4	1	300
18. Cane work	2	800	8	6,400	6	2	12,800
Total	35	18,108	8	1,80,596	7	65	2,72,552

(Vanamala, 2003, Table 11, p. 82)

This income worked out to 0.58 per cent of the total village agricultural gross value[6] in the 1995-96 year. The ratio of male and female earnings works out to 0.62: 0.58 or the male earnings are higher than that of female earnings despite their long hours on multi-works. This gap further widened by 2009-10 when most of the female occupations disappeared and many of the male occupations got up graded and restructured. Some of the male occupations like carpentry, piggery and washing clothes disappeared. Male occupations like village washermen have turned into washermen for industries as the state provided them with Dhobi Ghats. The barber profession shifted to haircutter saloon in fast urbanizing village. The number of grocer shops that engaged men have increased in number (Table 13). Against these changes in male occupations, no new occupations emerged to employ the displaced female workers. These changes indicate that nature of development adopted that has uprooted female labour forcing them to become housewives.

When the opportunities for women to work were shrinking very fast, the households have taken up construction of houses for earning rental incomes as a good deal. The data on construction shows that it was growing very fast as they accrued money either from sale of crop land or acquisition of it by the state. The cultivators turned phase-wise into rent earners. This has become a significant source for non-farm income seekers. The trends in house construction over a period has been progressing as follows.

House construction: The analysis on the sample data collected in 1995-96 (Vanamala, 2003, Table 7, p. 79) shows that 35 per cent of the houses owned by the respondent was constructed by his father and eight per cent by his grandfather. After the changes in the economy, more than 55 per cent of the farmer households constructed houses with the money accrued by sale of a part of their farm land. The second round of house construction was taken up in 2009-10. The data shows in this 50 per cent additional families from the total households in the village built slab (pacca) houses and owned more than one and sometimes even three houses.[7] The data on the house construction in the second round is presented in Table (15).

The sample data shows the source of finance for construction of these houses is only land sale/acquisition. It also shows (also in various contexts of this work) that none of these house of households had economic capacity other than the sale of land for construction of the slab house.

The details on finances drawn by the sample households for construction of the house shows that more than 98 per cent house builders did it from land sales. The data is given in Table 12.

Table 15: House Construction by Respondents by Selling Farm Land in 2009-10

Caste	*No. of Households*	*Percent*	*Type of House*					
			Pucca House	*Percent*	*Tiled Houses*	*percent*	*Sheet House*	*Percent*
SC	46	22.7	17	13.4	24	26.1	5	21.7
BC	139	57.6	65	51.2	56	60.9	18	78.3
FC	57	19.7	45	35.4	12	13.0	0	0.0
Total	242	100	127	100.0	92	100.0	23	100

Collected from the field from Gram Panchayat records.

borrowings from banks shows that no household has borrowed finance for construction except to meet some shortfalls. Another two per cent of households are those who voluntarily retired from industry. This shift of productive assets from farm land to house for rent seeking excluded women from productive work on land into domestic confines as housewife. From a role of production and earning her role turned into a dependent rent- seeking and reproduction as housewife (see Table 12). As the village is merged in the Greater Municipality the house property taxes have gone up making a dent in their incomes. This is how the capital is making its own way for its expansion. Along with this accumulation process the state also adopted the cost cutting method.

The house property has been used by the government to exclude these families from the benefits of welfare programmes showing them in upper income slabs. The state policy on Public Distribution is modified and that excludes the owners of slab houses from the eligibility of Rs 2 per kg rice under the scheme.

These changes affected women's freedom. Thus the production economy turned into rent-seeking economy in several ways.

The sample data shows that one of the new non-farm occupations emerged (after the late 1990s) out of the sale of farm land was driving four-wheelers on rent. The data in Table (13) shows that nine respondents purchased four wheelers for livelihood support. This works out to 13 per cent of households in the village. The vehicle owners stated that they could not rely totally on vehicles for earning regular livelihood incomes. Even if one assumes the vehicle earns good income the savings out of this income will not buy another vehicle once it becomes scrap. Another vehicle, for instance, the purchaser of a tractor is finding it difficult to keep the tractor engaged for the entire year on account of non-affordability of rents of tractors by the cultivators and not using them (Rs 1,000 per hour for the tractor). The technology of tractors is efficient and can till one acre of land in one hour. The data on land holdings shows 83% of the farmers do not have that much land holding to use tractor. Although this non-farm occupation with trucks and vans, earn a reasonably good income, they are not sufficient to buy a new vehicle after their life. These are also rental incomes and not incomes earned out of production. However these non-farm occupations exclude female labour from labour market and turn them into housewives. The empirical evidence on housewives shows that it has been consistently increasing (see Table 16).

Table 16: Purchase of Four Wheelers by Selling the Crop Land in 2009-10

Caste	*No. of hh*	*Per cent*	*Car hh*	*Per cent*	*Tractor*	*Truck*	*Per cent*	*Van*	*Per cent*
SC	46	16.1	1	7.1	0	0	0.0	0	0.0
BC	199	69.8	8	57.1	3	3	100.0	0	0.0
FC	40	14.0	5	35.7	0	0	0.0	3	100.0
Total	285	100.0	14	100.0	3	3	100.0	3	100.0

Source: Data collected from the field
hh = house holds

Table 17: The Number of Housewives in Working Age Group

Caste	*1979-80*	*1989-90*	*1995-96*	*2009-10*
SCs	3	14	41	150
BCs	63	63	95	210
FCs	32	50	72	120

Source: Vanamala, 2003, ICSSR Report

The data shows that during the year 1979 to 2009-10 the number of housewives in all social groups have been increasing (Table 17). This indicates that there are no new work opportunities for them to work. This is evident from the increasing number of housewives even from SCs which was the community with the highest participation in the work (the first survey) from their working age group. This has been increasing from three in the year 1979-80; rose to 14 in 1989-90 and further to 41 in 1995-96 and touched 150 by 2009-10. The majority community the BC women who were engaged in farming, were also forced to become housewives. The housewives swelled from 63, increased to 95 in 1989 and further rose to 210 by 2009-10 in the relevant age group. Among FCs also the same trend is seen. It was 32 in 1979-80 went up to 120 by 2009-10. The status of female labour that want to work to realize their productive capabilities were pushed into household reproduction services which has low social esteem.

Development is defined as shifting surplus labour from low (productivity) wage to higher (productivity) wage sector- the industries. The following data on industrial employment of the female labour that were displaced for the very purpose of development of industries in the region shows as follows.

Non-farm employment in Industries: The data on industrial employment of the labour from the village shows that only a small number of 166 male and (Vanamala, 2003, Table 18, p. 84) negligible 08 female could secure work. This works out to nine and 0.5 per cent of the population of the village respectively in 1995-96 (Vanamala, 2003). The flexible employment policy after the 1990s made all industrial work insecure. Female workers got downgraded as they have been employed only on a compassionate basis on unskilled menial work. Further probing into the working conditions of the male and female labour in the industries to see the differences in quality of life and conditions of work compared to the earlier position is necessary.

The data on the male workers working in industries in 1995-96 shows that they were paid consolidated wages at the rate of Rs 1200 per month. The employment was on contract basis and engaged for eleven months. After 11 months they are laid down and they have to wait for re-recruitment or look for fresh openings. And wages paid to female labour are at the rate of Rs 800 to 900 per month. Thus an industry where working conditions should be much better over that of agricultural employment shows no difference. Moreover in industrial employment also the wage difference continued to exist as in the agricultural sector. The decent employment is a distant dream. Out of 77 male workers, 22 were on skilled jobs (see Table 15). Quite a contrast to this data none of the female workers were on skilled jobs. Even these insecure and indecent opportunities shrunk over a period. The data shows that the number employed in industries from the village got reduced further from 166 to 77 male and from 09 to 08 between 1995-96 and 2009-10. The wages paid to unskilled casual male workers was Rs 3,000 and for skilled contract workers was Rs 5,000 per month. Against these payments in 2009-10 the permanent workers were paid Rs 10,000 per month prior to the 1990s. The data shows that the wages paid under the contract system are deflated to 1/3rd to ½ of the salaries paid to permanent workers in 1995-96.

The empirical observation shows that female employment particularly for unskilled workers was downgraded more into indecent and vulnerable conditions. The payments in export-oriented, manufacturing industries working with automatic technology are different from the industries working under subcontracting, piece rate systems. There was no uniform pattern in payments of wages among industries that employed female labour. A set of female labour intensive industries that were launched in the decade after 2000, shows that the wages paid were on a piece rate basis and very exploitative.

The non-farm employment in the labour market for female labour shows that 49 per cent of them are engaged in precarious labour work (Annexure 9). The most acclaimed MGNREGP[8] programme introduced measurement of work done with a lot of lacunae. For instance, despite the policy statement to avoid proclymers it is used on the ground that the soil identified for MGNREGP work is loose and cannot be allotted to workers. The amount paid as wages was decimal (this can be seen in the case studies mentioned by farmers).

These workers at present are diverted to work for corporate contractors in laying of the Ring Road. The contractor mud by digging 300-400 feet deep from the farm lands of these people for his project work. These farm lands are rendered useless for generations to come. This is the emerging scenario on female employment in the modern sector.

NOTES

1. Production of crops like sorghum, maize and ragi were for subsistence.
2. After the natural resources are destroyed for various reasons the cultivation (Table 11) slipped under bore-well irrigation. This irrigation is dependent on electricity power. With this it became a costly input over natural irrigation. The mono crops needed repeated applications of higher quantities of costly market inputs along with water. At this critical time the enforcement of SAP in agriculture (after 1991) resulting in withdrawal of state investments on irrigation and infrastructure against prioritization of the 40 industries proved a menace to agriculture.
3. **The strategies of sharing;** It is very significant to observe that the free power supply by the state for seven hours a day for cultivation, either the land is not sufficient under the bore-well or the water supply is not sufficient for land existing under the bore-well. To balance such conditions the farmers are forced to invent new methods of viable cultivation systems. The new joint cultivation (see point no. 10 above) is one such invention of the farmers which results in the scale up of production.

4. The survival strategy of this section of cultivators became Pluriactivity. This means men take up the non farm work and women work on the farm.
5. Misra (2000) observes that female labour participation in MGNREGP was 40% in Andhra Pradesh.
6. The data in Table (10) further confirms this argument that those who did not have land could not build their houses. This section of the households constitute 78 per cent and 22 per cent from BCs and SCs respectively. These live in sheeted houses.
7. **The data in Table (3) shows that by 2009-10 the fallow holdings (Padav) have increased to more** than 34% of the total number of holdings. Most of them are marginal holdings. Such holdings are dug to a depth of more than 200 feet by for laying the Ring Road. This crop land is a permanent loss for cultivation. The owners of these lands who sold earth to contractors worked as labour under the very same contractor as MGNREGP labour 46. Women had 33% reservation in MGNREGP; respondents asked whether this reserved employment brings them the social dignity that they had as cultivators?

4

The Farmers Speak: Profiles from the Field

The profiles of farmers cover all classes, castes and gender and impacts that affected them differently.

Case 1: Satyanarayana Sharma: Aged 50 years, completed Veda Pandit course. He was the former sarpanch and chairman of the rural agricultural cooperative bank from the Brahmin community, owns 10.32 acres of agricultural land. He says that his brothers and his own share of land which comes to a total of 20.24 acres of consolidated holding is jointly cultivated by him to upgrade cultivation to economic scale. This cultivation has been under sharecropping (till the year 2011). After sharecropping was withdrawn he turned into totally wage labour dependent farmer. He complains that the work culture has been sabotaged with speculative business. The MGNREGA, in his opinion promoted the culture of how to escape hard work. He further maintained that these labourers hardly work for one to one and a half hours as the in-charge is not able to provide sufficient work. SHG, DWCRA inculcated the culture of credit consumption without the previous hard work culture. He expressed his anguish with labour shortage in the previous year. He could not find labour for harvesting his wheat crop. The grain got dried and went waste. He had to burn the sugarcane crop due to the same reason of labour shortage. Because of the labour problem he stated, he shifted to traditional crops like wheat and onions. He held that the days have changed and now the cultivation sustains only in those families where there is their own labour. He stated that, he maintained all traditional infrastructure to support the sharecrop tenant. Sharecropping is pushed out of practice. He maintained that he cultivates the 'Desi' (or non-hybrid crops) despite its low yields of 10 to 12 bags per acre compared to 40 bags of hybrid. He adopted traditional technology for dry crops productions since his bore-well got dried. He stated that he has no labour and no water but he has access to capital as a former chairman in a cooperative agricultural credit society. Therefore he raised a crop loan of Rs 40,000 from the bank. The cultivation is crippled because of insufficient electricity supply, low prices for produce. The mills purchase the produce at low prices when the crop is not ready for harvest. Many farmers are selling such crops to protect themselves from the uncertainties and risks. He declared that with these problems of the cultivators the millers are benefited more than the farmers. Thus he said that the cultivation is becoming a losing proposition from all sides. He mentioned that the farmer is struck in a situation where he cannot escape but going ahead with cultivation. He stated that the farmer cannot afford to keep his land fallow. Keeping fallow works out costlier than raising crop with loss. He grew grass for his life-stock to keep the land occupied and sold off 13 acres for real estate. He also bought 10 acres of land in a neighbouring district where the problems are relatively less. He has specified a big list of the village service groups which were distributed land by the patwari and village elders in the early 1970s. Out land for doing village services. He said only Muslims and Temple land is retained. Others like ten households of band players, pothuraju household (who dance in the procession of goddess), barbers, dhobis, potters, blacksmiths and carpenters, begaris in-charge of cremation. Now these services are monetized. In such conditions how can cultivation be sustained? was his question. He said that unemployed are not finding any work, that resulted in increasing incidence of theft. The idle mind he observed has fanned the caste feelings. He has utter contempt for real estate business "even the ***labour***

class" is doing the real estate business. He observed that "the forefathers of these youth acquired and maintained the land assets for generations. Now these youth are selling the land and investing the money in speculative business". Earnings of this youth turned uncertain and depend on earnings of women in such times. He is angry with the state for its indifference to all these problems.

Case 2: Narasimha Reddy: former patwari aged 75 years, and he and his wife studied up to the 7th class. Both sons completed SSC and his daughters-in-law who completed degrees are housekeepers.

He owns two acres of cultivable land which he inherited from the family. Neither did he sell nor add any farm land and kept the land fallow for the last five years. This land is under tank which is silted fully. He uses this land to raise a crop loan of Rs 5,000 regularly to invest in the "travels"- started by his sons who do not know anything about cultivation.

He said he is happy with their venture in travels. He thinks because of development of the industries around their village, they could start the business of *travels* and feels that it is an opportunity for them to rise in economic status. However he mentioned that these industries were supported by the cultivators only to produce chemical fertilizers and pesticides that are required for their cultivation. He asserts that his own health at 75 years and his mother at 100 years is good and they do not use any medicines. While his wife, daughters and daughters-in-law, cannot survive without medicines. He believes that the secret of their health was that they ate food produced with well water without using chemical fertilizers and pesticides. He also believes that water drawn from wells with bullock power for irrigation of food crops early in the morning from four o' clock till sunrise, has a specific medicinal transmission to the crops. This kept their health in good condition.

He observes that the present generation is not interested in cultivation although the productivity increased by 10 times.

He resents the indifference of the present state that is silent on conversion of cultivable land into plots which left only 20% of land under cultivation in the village. He is equally unhappy with the indifference of the government towards pollution which harmed even mango orchids which are not growing beyond two feet height after three years. People incurred a loss of Rs 3,000 in the production of paddy on each acre. He cited the case of a former Sarpanch who raised 25 quintals@Rs 1,700 and sold for Rs 42,500. His expenditure on inputs itself was Rs 45,000 which led to a loss of Rs 3,000. He is upset about industrial pollution that affected 80 per cent of the land in the village.

He also observed that cultivators are unable to maintain the livestock necessary for their cultivation (it has become costly affairs). Due to unaffordability of the cost they keep their land fallow or selling it and joining industrial work force.

Case 3: Asaiah: aged 62 years, munnurkapu, completed 7th class, lives in a joint family engaged in agriculture. He was a ***land revenue collector (maskuri) under patwari and shifted to Gram Panchayat (GP)***. He has a son who also studied upto the 7th class and turned into a cultivator.

Asaiah is paid Rs 2350 per month by the Gram Panchayat. He owns nine (9) acres of farm land. Out of it four acres is sunk in tank silt, the other five acres is dry land under a single crop. Two acres of land is under double crop. Six acres of land was purchased by him 30 years back from a neighbour with the help of Patwari.

He believed that he has sufficient land and work to engage his entire family. His wife and son are engaged in cultivation work for about 10 months in a year. Their cultivation is labour intensive. They do not get time to even visit relatives. He owns all agricultural tools including two bullocks, three buffaloes. He hires agricultural machines only in emergency. Out of five bore wells that he tried, one is working. He wants to get the other bores repaired but there is no assistance from any corner.

He has raised Rs .60,000 crop loan from a cooperative

society at 12 per cent rate of interest per annum which is of help as the money lender charges higher rate of interest. He says that while there is increase in production but swallowed by the rising input costs. Although his crop is covered under crop insurance that never was useful for the protection of their crops. Same is the case with livestock, and gave up insuring the lifestock.

He says that rise of land prices has been oppressive. While he could purchase six acres of land 30 years ago now his son cannot add any land as the prices are exorbitant. This made many young cultivators shift to non-farm work. .He strongly feels that the youth should take an interest in agriculture and work hard. He lives in a 100-year-old tile-roofed house. He neither sold any land nor constructed a new house. He stores his produce in his own house and markets it from there in retail to the migrant households. This time he complains that produce remained unsold for the last eight months. He questions the state policy and asks when we are growing rice in the village why does the government import it from other states for public distribution incurring transport costs unnecessarily?

On the social change front although Asaiah has not sold any land, he has gifted his ancestors' property to his daughter which was unthinkable some time ago.

Asiah discussed the other points of his personal life. His wife is suffering from heart disease and got operated with the help of the Arogyasree card. Politically he is quite aware of the changes that are taking place in the village.

This respondent cultivates with family labour keeping excess land fallow. He is unable to cultivate his entire land as his son does not like his daughter-in-law working on land and his wife is sick. He had to engage wage labour that works out costlier.

Case 4: K. Veeranna, aged 35 years. He is illiterate and belongs to the Kummary (potter man) caste. His family is engaged in agriculture.

Veeranna says that the state has taken away his four acres

of land for expansion of the ring road and also lost the animals that were bought by his father because of the grazing problem. He is left with 30 guntas under the tank. He could not purchase any new land on account of unaffordable prices. He recounts that his grandfather had two acres, his father bought three more acres making it 5 acres, in his own time it went down to 0.30 guntas. He added that he was paid compensation Rs one lakh per acre. He used this money for construction of a house which he has let out and earns a rent of Rs 3600 pm. This is his monthly income for his livelihood. With the remaining compensation money he cleared old debts, performed a death ceremony, shared some amount with his sister and a small amount was kept in a fixed deposit.

He cited several limitations for cultivation of this fertile piece of land which was under a tank. He raised 25 bags of paddy in a single crop. If he had a bore well he would have raised a second crop. He is upset that the seeds distributed at subsidized rates by the agricultural cooperative society hardly germinate rendering the cultivation into unsustainable occupation. He further adds that the state failed in effectively implementing the agricultural policies. He is also unhappy about his inabilities to use his own labour in cultivation as he injured his leg. He is hiring a tractor for tilling and harvesting. He employed 'adda' labour (labour market) knowing well that it is costly and such labour do not co-operate in the work.

He is illiterate and worried about the fact that he is not being imparted only son of his parents, he never had an opportunity to learn any skills. He feels sad that his traditional caste occupation of pot making lost its marketability. There is no common land left to get clay for making pots.

When he was asked why he did not go to a doctor for treatment, he replies that he was poor as he has "more daughters whom he has to feed and they are still young". As this community is generally well-off, the dowry rate is high which makes him feel that the girl children are a burden to bring up (marking the sustenance of patriarchic domination).

Case 5: Pottolla Narsimlu: Aged 46. Education 10th; caste Madiga; joint family, contract supervisor in Gram Panchayat and earns Rs 1,900 per month. He has four grown up children, One studied upto the inter and works in an engineering college in the village as attender for a salary of Rs 1,800. The other three are pursuing their studies. One is doing BEd, one is in the intermediate and the fourth is in the eighth class. The respondent says the education of his children has become possible because of government institutions. He states that along with the contract work in the Gram Panchayat he also cultivates land. He owns 20 guntas of wet, assigned land under the bore well. He has also purchased five guntas of additional land 20 years back. It is a single crop cultivable. His wife works both as family labour (for 20 days) and hired labour for four months a year. He produces 12 bags of paddy, 10 kgs of sorghum and tomatoes. Except for tomato, other crops are for self-consumption. He has no cattle or tools and implements for cultivation. He hires machines and a tractor for this purpose. He raised a crop loan of Rs 28,000 from the rural cooperative society @12% interest. He says he could cultivate because of subsidized credit, seeds, fertilizers and electricity charges. However sometimes the seeds supplied are of poor quality. Since he got a house in the government housing scheme, he did not sell farm land to build a house. Before he joined the Gram Panchayat, he worked in the industry of Hyderabad Lamps for a payment of Rs 1,800 pm. The industry was closed without informing the workers without paying any compensation. He found fault with the government for such a decision and allowed all political parties to intervene in the matters of labour problems, the representatives from TDP, BJP and Congress were on the industrial advisory board. He says that these politicians are paid regularly by industrialists in the name of service as labour advisors. The politicians and industrialists have nexus against the labour. He thinks because of this reason that the industrialists dared to close industries without any care for the displaced labour. To a question that what can be done for the improvement of his conditions in cultivation, he replied that repair of bore-wells and supplying of subsidized fertilizers. The respondent is politically informed. He knows that the government has created the NREGP to generate employment for the labour, his wife and mother worked under the programme. They have earned Rs 60, Rs 50, Rs 40 as their wages which are less than even minimum wages. Such programmes are made, he thinks, only to benefit the commission agents who cheated the labour. The respondent observed that his wife is a SHG member and availed of a loan twice, once Rs 10, 000 and another time Rs 20,000. This helped them in meeting their financial needs.

He says, "I have knowledge but no money. And those who got jobs they have a better changing lifestyle. Those who do not have any assets went for education and are leading a good life. Those who do not have these two assets—education and a job— their life turned miserable". He maintained that "in the old days the poor depended on the Patel, now they are on their own. The life style is made individual-centric. Either for education or for jobs one cannot depend on the government." These feelings are a comment on the nature of the present model of development. It is clear that this model withdrew state support under global pressure. That publicly funded education played an important role in shaping the lives of poor and dalit people. His children are in a government school which is a part of the social welfare scheme. With higher aspirations, a majority of the families are sending their children to private schools which are robbing people of their small earnings. This case shows "unless there is state support for cultivation or for education, or other welfare supports, it is impossible for people to improve their lives and living conditions."

Case Studies on Female-Headed Cultivator

Case 6. Kalagoni Bhayamma is a cultivator from a BC Shepherd (Kurma) caste aged 27 years. She is maternally related to her mother-in-law who is aged of 50 years. Bhayamma's husband and father-in-law died of a heart attack. Bhagyamma has a son. Both widows aspire to educate him in English medium. This general perception that education in English medium to children opens better opportunities. They spend most part of their earnings to ensure a better future for her son.

This family has two acres of ancestral property. This land has been left for cultivation after Bhagyamm's father-in-law sold ten acres for construction of a house to earn rent. They get rent of Rs .2400 per month. From the beginning paddy was the only crop raised by this household. Now they have diversified into cash crops to meet the regular cash needs which the respondent says have gone up. The mother-in-law sells head load of vegetables within the village. If more vegetables are produced they sell them in the neighbouring industrial centre. Thus the cash crop production in varied seasons and head load marketing has increased the work load of female members. These women work on multiple livelihood activities. They take up wage labour work whenever they do not have work on their own land. This is again to earn cash.

Bhayyamma's mother-in-law says that she is not finding any problems in getting inputs and credit. The credit amount allotted by the cooperative credit bank stands at Rs .10,000 per acre. This entire money that she was eligible for has not been borrowed. Some amount is deferred. This is to save on interest. The structure of the cooperative society has no facility for second borrowing when needed. Therefore she borrows from moneylenders by mortgaging her jewellery. Although she takes this loan at a higher rate of interest, she thinks this is wiser. This means that the cooperative credit is designed to meet the requirements of farmers based on their nature of work. If a loan is given in a fixed time in the year as has been done, it is not suitable for the changed cropping pattern. Therefore, to meet the changes in cropping pattern and the increased social cash needs, the respondent is raising a loan from moneylenders. They want small amounts for different farm activities at different times.

Bhagyamma's mother-in-law has three daughters. For the first daughter 100 grams of gold as dowry was given. (Earlier this caste used to offer herds of sheep as dowry). By the time of the second daughter's marriage the market prices gone up and she had to give Rs 1.5 lakhs as dowry. For the third daughter it was two lakhs. These daughters celebrate their children's birthdays and expect gifts from their mother. The adoption of this culture gradually gives in to commoditization of rural agrarian culture. The returns from land and incomes used to be in a fixed season per year. Now the cash requirements of the families are raised and are more frequent.

This female-headed family sells paddy from their residence as she thinks that the rice mills cheat them with their tricks. The tricks like demanding the farmers to dry the paddy more than the usual way before it is taken to the mill. They also impose several coats of polish to the rice. She maintains that this causes a lot of weight loss in rice. Therefore they prefer to sell it in retail from their residence to local buyers.

The independent cultivation of paddy by women is made possible with mechanization of tilling. The tilling is a strictly male activity. The respondent hires a tractor for preparing the land for paddy. The independent bullock farming is turned into tractor/market dependent activity. The respondent says that using a tractor has become unavoidable because of the higher scale of production which has become possible because of use of high yielding variety seeds. If higher level production is not raised savings are not possible in the cultivation. With lower level production with bullock economy, she says, it is impossible to save anything even for self-consumption.

The tractor tilling and high yielding variety compels the cultivators to engage wage labour. Technically transplantation and tilling with a tractor should take place simultaneously to avoid any hardening of soil which makes transplantation difficult. For this reason paddy crop has become wage labour dependent and labour intensive. Its cultivation is also strictly season based. Because of these reasons this household engages the labour for transplantation. For weeding on the third day of transplantation they spray anti-weed chemicals. The diversification into vegetable cultivation (cash crop) also demands heavy human labour making cultivation labour intensive. To reduce production costs on labour weeding which has to be done four times, they do weeding work by themselves. The tasks of female labour changed along with the farm technology, cropping pattern and crops.

The tasks associated with cultivation were dependent on use value. The respondent stated that thirty years ago the wages for paddy cultivation were paid in kind after 20 to 25 days of work. In those days women on their way back home from the farm used to collect green grass for their livestock, green vegetables for their own consumption, wood for fuel, etc. She further observes that at present these activities have disappeared completely. For instance, there is hardly any livestock left in the village. There is no need for grass. She maintains that the grass on boundaries has grown into bushes which turned into hideouts for the snakes. Another activity of this type was organic manure spreading. During its spread on farm land women were collecting waste wood lying on farm land to use as cooking fuel. As the present cooking is shifted to kerosene stoves, collection of fuel disappeared.

Making paddy sprouts and spreading them on the farm were female activities. That has been shifted to wage labour. The wages vary between Rs 130 to Rs 250 per day based on work pressure of female agricultural labour. Along with wages a packet of local liquor became a part of wages. She observed that when the labour consume liquor they do not feel like collecting green vegetables. She expressed that the entire production activities for use value have turned into exchange value.

The difficult task of the female-headed cultivator is the protection of the motor kept in the paddy field during nights and also the problem to use the subsidized electricity supplied at night.

Case 7: Amma: Amma's husband the late Reddy, died in an accident four years back, while he was engaged in milk business. She is survived by two daughters and a son. The elder daughter's marriage was performed by her husband and the son-in-law is a drunkard. Another daughter was eloped by a landlord family. The son is studying in the 8th class. She has a tiled old house. One room is let out for Rs 300 pm. Amma suffers from epilepsy.

Her father gifted her two acres of land which is under a bore well with sufficient water. She says that this scarce water resource tempts her to continue the cultivation. However she is sad that she could not buy a motor which has become a problem for cultivation. She is not getting a tenant for sharecropping because of this problem.

Amma borrows a crop loan from the rice miller at a rate of interest of Rs 36 per cent per annum. She says she has to sell the produce only to him as she borrows from him. She says she is also compelled to work on these two acres for raising paddy crop along with the sharecroppers as free labour on account of acute labour shortage, particularly of female agricultural labour. She thinks that contribution of her labour works as incentive for share cropper. This reminds us about the landlord providing bullocks and tools to attract tenants, while the same is done by a female-headed cultivator by extending her free labour. This indicates the new dimension of the female production role.

The experience of Amma with paddy production in the present year is quite revealing. She said that 42 bags of paddy were raised in her one acre of land. The price paid per bag was Rs 900. This worked out to Rs 37,800 value added expenditure on this area worked out to Rs 31,100. This comes Rs 6,600 and net value. From this net value Rs 540 interest is paid to the sharecropper/(miller who lent the crop loan). Her take home value of production works out to Rs 5,520. She adds that on the whole for her labour and rent of her land she gets two bags of rice. This is a clear case of exploitation of a vulnerable widow.

Owning property by a woman is rare in a patriarchical society. This sometimes leads to psychological problems. Amma thinks that to appropriate her property anti-social elements keep harassing her. She adds that people play witchcraft by keeping a lemon and head part of a dead goat on the threshold of their house. This is done she says to make her run away from the village. This explains her feeling of insecurity for owning property.

This is a sad case of a female-headed cultivator. Amma's daughter eloped by landlord's son. When she went to see her daughter, the landlord's son who had eloped her had not allowed Amma to see her daughter. They abused her and said that she has no rights over the girl, as she has not paid any dowry to her daughter to continue any relations with her. This Amma explains that the dowry payment, a patriarchical value is used against her to appropriate her property. Thus the land property and young daughter are commodities in the present day practice.

The Emerging Patterns: From the above case studies it is evident that the impact of the changes in agrarian policy is different on caste, class and on gender. To start with the small and marginal farmers were hit more with unviable holdings, unprecedented input price rise, low output prices, irregularities in quality of seeds, insufficient power supply and malpractices of millers. The small and marginal cultivators that continued cultivation turned their holdings into family holdings causing women shift from hired labour into family labour. This class was affected not only economically but also socially. The changes in macro policy affected children's education and health of the family members.

The wage-dependent cultivators were hit hard by the subsequent changes in the occupational shifts of female labour which turned into acute shortage of female agricultural labour. This pushed them to consolidate land to shift into commercial crops.

The case studies on female-headed households have shown trends in successful cultivation. They could meet their socio-economic demands. This is the hope for development of research and development that is oriented to female cultivators.

Another female-headed household who is a victim of greed of capital and hold of patriarchy indicated further policy efforts for protection of female labour cultivator that that is vulnerable.

Conclusions

The study on commercialization of crops to commoditization of farm land shows that there were 1991 acres of land under the village in 1984-85. Out of it only 18 acres or (which works out to less than one percent) was not used for cultivation. The remaining of 99 per cent of land was put to cultivation and this part of the land was recorded as 'KABIL KASTU', "meaning fit for cultivation". Out of it 1671.35 acres were developed with water resources (wet land). The irrigation tanks cover 195.36 acres, 31.25 acres was covered under water storage channel (kuntas), 75.11 acres was covered under backwaters of rivers and the rest of the land was covered under wells (collected from the Gram Panchayat office). This huge infrastructure for water resources was the primary condition for the paddy cultivation.

The paddy was cultivated in 1200 acres in Kharif and 200 acres in the Rabi season in the village. The crop is further pushed towards female labour intensive that engaged extensive female labour with commercialization of paddy crop. The state promoted extensively the Green Revolution package that enhanced paddy crop intensity, productivity and area under paddy crop (area increased both by distribution of government land, shift of land under dry crops). The study shows that it engaged male and female cultivators in the ratio 2:97 and the agricultural labour in the ratio of 0.60:1. This triggered the expansion in female farm employment.

The study shows that about 83 per cent of wet land was in distribution in the land slab of 1-2.5 acres. Another 11 per cent of land was in distribution in the land slab of 2.6-5 acres. The minimum holding size of wet land was in the land slab of 1-2.5 acres in the village even up to 1995. It is also very significant that the land rich that own more than 20 and above acres had mere 0.43 per cent of wet land. This explains that rich owned mostly dry land.

The study explains that because of this minimum size and rich water resources there was high rigidity in the sale of land. The study shows that the land sales in the village started only with acquisition of land under public use. This was acquired for launching the public sector undertakings under the **development of this backward region** for **Gareebi Hatao** (political agenda of Indira Gandhi). The total land sold in a period of more than 20 years between the years 1973-74 to 1990-91 it was a mere 160 acres or 12% of total land of the village. Out of it 37 acres were acquired for industries. This industrialization inspired real estate business and has shifted 48 acres under real estate business. The remaining 75 acres or 50 per cent sales that changed the ownership was relocated in the village by purchases of village cultivators. Thus the study revealed that the farm land dependent occupation had strong roots among the village cultivators.

These two state interventions to start with (commercialization of paddy and industrialization with public sector undertakings that absorbed several members from landed households) along with rich rural non-farm occupations, that engaged 648 male and 585 female in the ratio 1: 1.107 made the paddy cultivation profitable. For instance, 48 per cent of the households were earning as high an income of Rs 5,000-10,000 per annum. Another 18 per cent and 11 per cent of the households were earning an income of Rs 10,001-15,000 and 15,001-25,000 per annum respectively and those that earn over Rs 30,000 per annum were two per cent households. Only 20 per cent of the households were earning a lower level income of Rs 2,001-5,000 per annum during 1979-80s.

This prosperity reached a point where the culture as a push factor operated on the increase in incomes of the households to push female wage labour into homes to get confined to domestic reproduction—a process of "Housewifization". For instance, the process is reflected in the following distribution of hired labour.

The study shows from the Rs 0-1,000 income per annum category of the household the female hired labour constitute as high as 88 percent, while in the income category of above Rs 15,000 PA there were no female hired labour. This relationship of hired labour with caste and level of income reveal interesting results. From forward castes households there are no instances of hired labour after Rs 5,000 and above income PA while the hired labour was 100 per cent from these households where the income slab was of Rs 1,000 and below PA. This data shows that the forward caste women were withdrawn from hired labour once the household crosses an income of Rs 5,000 PA. From the backward castes and scheduled castes, there was no hired labour after the household crossed Rs 10,000 and Rs 15,000 respectively.

The study shows subsequent to this prosperity on paddy cultivation a high level shift of farm land to non-farm was started particularly in the holdings of small and marginal farmers. The study revealed that there was an unprecedented strategic rise in input prices (chemical fertilizers, pesticides, water, electricity), land prices and in prices of agricultural services (like services of tractor) against this, there was depressed prices of agricultural output, distribution of fake agricultural seeds and non-cooperation of rice mills in levy paddy purchases, from cultivators state imports of paddy from other states for supply through Public Distribution system together made paddy cultivation unviable. This was further added with withdrawal of state support in infrastructural development particularly in water resource development which was appropriated by industries. These changes at policy level pushed the paddy cultivation into a deep crisis. These market conditions forced the small and marginal farmers to sell their holdings that turned into unviable. The land sales are reflected in shrinking land holdings.

For instance, the study shows that the dry land slab of less than one acre did not exist during 1995-96. By 2009-10 about 10 per cent of total dry land fell into this land slab. In the subsequent upper slab of 1-2.5 acres, 70 per cent of dry land was under distribution among the households. It also fell to 43 per cent by 2009-10. This explains the fact that the farm holding size of marginal and small farmers was shrinking to a size that turned into unviable for cultivation. These unviable holdings resulted in a drastic shift into either to fallows or into sales in the land market. This resulted in forced shift of female labour into non-farm occupations. Against these shifts of land holdings and female labour in the small and marginal cultivators, this study unfolded a dialectic strategy adopted by the wage-dependent cultivators that have consolidated land holdings and converted them into commercial cultivation to escape from the crisis of acute shortage of female agricultural labour. This is clear from the direction of the land mobility.

The dry land slab of 2.6 to 5 acres was 16 per cent in 1995-96. It increased to more than 26 per cent by 2009-10. The area in the subsequent slab of 5.1 to 10 has increased from about seven per cent to 21 per cent that works out to three times of its area existed in 1995-96. This upward mobility of land explains that from small farmers the land shifted to wage-dependent cultivators. The mobility in wet land also exhibited the same trend.

The distribution of wet land I, II shows 95 and 98 per cent of their respective total was in the slab of 1-2.5 acres in 1995-96. This percentage in this slab was reduced to 54 per cent pushing down 17 per cent of it to a new slab of less than one acre. The remaining 24 per cent has moved to upward slabs. Only 17 per cent of the wet land area (earlier it was 95 percent) is in distribution among 67 per cent of the households. In the slab of 1-2.5 acres about 30 per cent of the households own 54 per cent of it. These two land slabs together constitutes 97 per cent of the households of the wetland holders. The ownership of wet holdings is very crucial from the point of view of employment for female labour. This has been reduced by displacing female labour from small and marginal holdings.

On the higher side of land slab of 10-20 acres of wet, about 13 acres is transferred to a single owner. This is a new development of land concentration in 2009-10. In the entire history of the village, at no point of time was this huge area of wet land was owned by any single family. This concentration of wet land displaced female labour on account of shifting of this land to commercial crops.

The study has shown that by 2009-10 the land remained with cultivators was 237 acres. Out of it 17 per cent is owned by 57 per cent of the landed households in the land slab of less than one acre. Another 32 per cent of households owned 41 per cent of land in the slab of 1-2-5. Yet another 11 per cent of households owned 35 per cent land in the slab of 2.6-5 acres. Seven per cent of land was owned by less than one per cent of households in 10-20 acres slab by 2009-10. By this time the number of small and marginal cultivators that survived in cultivation got reduced to 11 per cent of households compared to 80 per cent in the late 1970s. The per-household holding size fell to $1/4^{th}$ of the size that prevailed in 1999. Thus both the strategies of small and wage-dependent cultivators contributed to displacement of female labour. Such major changes in land transfers have transformed the social composition of land distribution across the social categories. The data suggests that although the area owned is small (1-2 and 2-5 acres) more number of households from BCs depended on land for livelihood. (The changes in cultivation also have taken up). The displacement of female labour simultaneously happened from non-farm occupations that were supporting agriculture.

The study has shown that the rural non-farm occupations supported with 0.62 per cent and 0.58 per cent of agriculture incomes by male and female earnings to each of the farm households and supplied cash investments for cultivation. Many of these traditional non-farm occupations that existed up to 1980 have disappeared. For instance, the application of chemical fertilizers caused erosion of sheep and goat non-farm occupation that enjoyed the highest economic and informal political power in the village economy.

The study revealed that the new non-farm works that emerged have displaced female labour from the production role. Most of occupations emerged were "rent-seeking" that did not provide any role for female labour and forced them to become housewives. The study has shown that the female labour even from SCs and BCs that had the highest share in labour also had to turn into fast increasing "housewifization".

This change the role of female labour from that of production to housewife is a deterioration in her status from producer to a dependent.

The most trusted field for economists for creating productive non-farm employment is industries. The study shows that though the region had developed into one of the biggest industrial estates in Asia, it could not provide work opportunities to these displaced village female labour. The industries have changed their employment policy from permanent recruitment into flexible employment. The industrial employment is made insecure and most exploitative particularly for female labour. The industrial employment was 'indecent' in terms of wage payments and in terms of quality of work created. Therefore because of this lack of non-farm opportunities, a fraction of farm households still continued with cultivation adopting cost reduction strategies.

The study revealed that the real value of paddy cultivation per acre is Rs 28,000. The total expenditure on labour, machinery and material on one acre of paddy cultivation worked out to Rs 31,100. This comes to Rs 3,100 loss on each acre of paddy cultivation.

This loss has been planned to reduce by substituting the family labour in paddy cultivation or by changing the crop.

In the cultivation of cost saving, the cultivators have reorganized land holdings to limit the cultivation by family labour, the family farm activities were reorganized (mechanized and manual), they have reallocated the intra-household division of farm work, re-mobilized resources and relocated the product markets and restructured the cropping patterns between food and commercial and low investment crops (the allocation of land for paddy crops has been reduced from 41.97 per cent in 1995-96, to about 39 per cent of total cultivated area in 2009-10. The paddy cultivation is substituted with other crops.). The adoption of these new strategies have changed the production roles of female labour. The role of female labour changed from hired labour to **female family farm labour** (unpaid labour), **feminized farm labour (by sliding down to low investment**

crops), pluri-activity female labour and female hired agricultural labour and additional farm activities (previously that were done either by male labour or by machine) have been roled on to female labour. The production roles turned into more marginalized.

The case studies have clearly brought out socio-cultural-economic transitions and policy impacts on female labour. The case studies reiterated that the minimalist model of development resulted in adverse effects on education and health of the rural people. The state policies that prioritized capital by creating feminized industrial employment, by creating land price bubble that resulted in speculative land business and consequently shift of crop land to non-farm business. The state policies like direct loan to tenants on tenancy land, shifting of labour enrolled under MGNREGP to corporate non-farm has resulted in an agricultural crisis.

The case studies brought out a clear picture of different impacts of the model of development on caste, class and gender. To start with the small and marginal farmers were hit more with unviable holdings, unprecedented input price rise, low output prices, irregularities in quality of seeds, insufficient power supply and malpractices of millers. The small and marginal cultivators that continued cultivation turned their holdings into family holdings to turn female labour into family labour. The wage-dependent cultivators were hit hard by the subsequent changes in the occupational shifts of female labour which turned into acute shortage of female agricultural labour. This pushed them to consolidate land to shift into commercial crops. The study has shown trends in successful and vulnerable cultivation by female cultivators by entering into cash crops along with the regular paddy. They could meet their socio-economic demands. This is the hope for development of research and development that is oriented to female cultivators. The study also throws light on greed of capital and hold of patriarchy on vulnerable female cultivators. Impacts are reflected in wage differences between males and females despite acute shortage of female agricultural labour. Therefore this model of development works for its own expansion and not for better conditions to female labour.

Suggestions to Policy Makers for Revival of Cultivation

One: Concerted policy efforts in all public policies in agriculture should be to focus on small and marginal farmer households with special reference to female employment towards clonomie and social dignity to them.

Two: Leasing-out and leasing-in land should be institutionalized. The cultivation for the aspiring women be made possible by channelizing three essential requirements namely—access to water, tractor services and to flexible soft credit.

Three: The policy should consider additional investments and maintenance of infrastructure and additions to irrigation and market linkages as critical inputs in sustenance of agriculture.

Four: The "new joint cultivation" should be institutionalized and promoted with necessary legal support. The female farmers associations, cooperatives and SHGs should be encouraged to take up cultivation in groups by sharing the resources and soft credit and for regular upgradation of skills and education in agricultural applications.

Five: The high land prices, the high input/low output prices push factors from cultivation should be regulated by the state intervention.

Six: The promotion of R&D in female-oriented technology in agriculture, and its dissemination of training in certain crops like paddy.

Seven: Diversification of crops, implementation of land reforms and supporting multi-livelihoods in the non-farm realm are some measures for expansion of productive employment to female labour.

Eight: The labour working under MGNREGP should be given rural non-farm work during the lean agricultural season,

Nine: The wages should be paid in kind through PDS. The PDS should be linked to farm produce of the farmers from the village. This solves two problems: the grain can be distributed at lower prices and farmers can get the remunerative price.

Ten: A village committee involving cultivators from various castes, classes and gender should be formed which decides the village development needs.

Some Theoretical Formulations

Economically unviable holdings get feminized into female family exploitative cultivation by marginalizing female tasks and generate manual additional unpaid female tasks in the context of loss of their identity as **workers**.

When cultivation feminizes the family turns into pluri-activity, the cost cutting on cultivation is imposed on female labour resulting in her *super exploitation.* This is an indicator of a sick society.

5

The Self-Help Groups (SHGs) in Andhra Pradesh State: An Empirical Case Study of a Village in Telangana

Introduction: In the_last chapter on agriculture and changes in female production roles shows that the labour that is displaced from farms tried to enter the new non-farm works. Most of the newly emerged non-farm works are such that they exclud female labour. For instance, livelihood occupations like four wheelers for hired work, construction of houses for rent seeking hiring on rent and, business of lifestock have excluded them from work to become housewives and get confined to reproduction work and to remain unemployed. By this time the Self-Help Group Movement picked up, these unemployed women were easily available for mobilization into it, as the state had already provided sufficient ground to boost the movement. At policy level it is stated and impressed that, the only potential employment available for the female labour is to set up micro enterprises by being a member of SHG for livelihood occupation.

The number of Self-Help Groups mobilized (SHG)[1] is largest in the state of Andhra Pradesh within the country. It is generally argued that the access to credit is one of the most useful financial tools available to the poor, credit allows human capital to be leveraged with physical capital in order to increase income and it serves as an insurance allowing consumption to be spread evenly across time.[2] With the background of such arguments the study focuses on the enquiry into functioning of the SHG and their potential support in providing productive employment for eradicating poverty and to lead life with social dignity.

The SHGs in the state can be categorized into two broad models. For the convenience of this study they are categorised as Private Microfinance Institutions and NGOs model, the Integrated Indira Kranthi Patham (IKP)[3] project model under registered Society—***Society for Elimination of Rural Poverty (SERP)*** which was launched in 2004-05 as an *Autonomous Society* with the World Bank and UNDP Funds. At present it is the single largest poverty alleviation project in South Asia and in the government of Andhra Pradesh. The other section of SHGs mobilized are under SGSY. They are meant for poverty alleviation through self-employment of youth and with cluster programmes focused on weaker sections of the society. It is operated by the District Rural Development Agency (DRDA) with the help of Block/Mandal development Officer, Banks, Panchayati Raj, technical institutions and NGOs. Yet another section of SHGs mobilized is under the Pavala Vaddi Programme. This programme is to be paid by the state government, the subsidy on the interest amounts charged by the bank on the loans they released to the SHG members against their savings. This subsidy works out to the interest rate charged as Rs 0.25 (paisa) on every rupee borrowed. This programme is also placed under the DRDA structure for operation.[4] These SHG models differ in their objectives, nature of financial composition, sources of finance. They also differ in administrative and organizational structures. The following presentation deals with the origin and source of finances for these institutions.

The SHGs were formed as thrift groups under the Project Velugu, in the state, with the subsidy component provided from the Rolling Funds of the Government of India programme called Swarna Jayanthi Swarojgar Yojana (SGSY), for self-employment of weaker sections in 1992.[5] These funds worked as a catalyst to expand the allocations by nationalized banks under the priority sector (peddled by the NABARD).[6] The Velugu and the subsequent Projects for poverty eradication—such as Andhra Pradesh Poverty Initiative Programme (2000-2006) and the Andhra Pradesh Poverty Reduction Project (APRPRP) (2002-2009) were all brought under the Society for Elimination of Rural Poverty (SERP). Now the SERP is working on this project of mobilizing SHGs. Along with these managerial changes in SHG, the financial reforms in the new market (liberalized and globalised) also introduced changes that affect the working of SHGs.

The Reserve Bank of India introduced "The Financial Inclusion Policy" by giving new financial sanctions for expansion of business of the national and international financial institutions. This spiralled a series of changes in the financial market like in 2005, the Government of India introduced the International Year of Micro Finance **(MFI)** in its **annual budget** with a sanction to the ***external*** commercial business. NABARD financed and launched a new programme called the **Bank Linkage Programme** authorizing the commercial banks to lend directly to the SHGs at the market rate of interest, subverting its rural credit obligation. The reforms have deregulated interest rates in the financial market.[7] Micro credit and micro enterprises were identified and encouraged by the government and financial markets as the core rural livelihoods[8]. The NGOs[9] that were started with philanthropic donations for serving the public cause under ***society*** or ***trust*** policy were sanctioned the Non-Bank-Finance Company status (NBFC) to have higher access to finances. The NGOs were also permitted to draw money from banks at a lower rate of interest for relending this to SHGs at a higher rate of interest. Thus the entire private financial sector underwent a metamorphic change and enjoyed freedom for full-swing business. The satisfaction of the financial business sections is expressed in the description that "*the policy environment in India (in AP in particular) has been extremely supportive for the growth of MFI (APMAS, 2005)". This is reflected in the magnitude of expansion of SHGs in AP*. In Andhra Pradesh there were 12 lakh SHGs in 2010-2011. It is the largest in number and has been growing significantly. The SHGs in the village under study are selected for case study with the specified objectives as follows.

Theoretical Frame for the Study on SHG: It is a widely accepted argument that the institution of SHG is created in the financial market to use as the levers of capital accumulation. The historical account of the Primitive Accumulation of Capital according to Milford Bateman (2010:30)[10] triggered with the *financialization wave* that started in 1973. This has introduced funded International NGOs to work on the political programmes like "Status of Women, Civil Rights, Labour Rights and Poverty Elimination." These NGOs lend the funds borrowed from the international agencies to SHG women at exorbitant interest rates. And these funds with recurring credit and debt spiralled upward that raises business to higher and higher levels. Bateman stated that *'this is precisely the central feature of contemporary capital and its accumulation process'*. He observed that such financial capital acquires power to construct its own hegemony (monopoly power) over the financial system for capital accumulation. In pursuit of this hegemony new institutional arrangements would also be done with the nexus of the state-finance. He stated that such a nexus functions as levers of speculation, predation, fraud and thievery'.

David Harvey (2005) argued that there is a fast rise in power of finance that has hastened the reforms into privatization and commercialization from 2003 in India. These reforms made easy the financial lending for consumption and for setting up of 'micro enterprises', in the name of poverty reduction from 2006. He adds that this lending for consumption was introduced to expand the business in micro finance. As the experience worldwide shows that the scope for consumption loan is as high as 90% of the finances lent to the poor. Thus the consumption lending that induced business expansion is known as "*Credit-Induced Effective Demand Model" (CIMFM)*. He analysed the tenets of financial lending and expansion of the business aimed by choosing women as its clients. He arrived at the ascribed reasons that it is aimed at women as *"women being best at repayment"*.

Haroon Habib (cited in Bateman 2011)[11] observed that the Micro Finance through SHGs for poverty alleviation has been supported by the United States, World Bank, world's powerful lobbies, "West Friends of Grameen" (NGO), Sa-Dhana-the Association of Community Development, etc. He also observed over a hundred micro finance practitioners participate in this business in India achieving financial monopoly. Therefore he calls Muhammad Yunus the founder of the microfinance model as the "villain" who contributed to economic vulnerability of the households with debt traps and dispossession[12] of their assets (Reddy Narasimha, 2007). He observed that in Bangladesh the women borrowers were pushed into 'poverty' and 'debt trap'. He substantiated this with the observations on the business performance of micro enterprises.

The micro enterprises on which the financial lending was emphasized, Bateman observed, were weak both financially and organizationally. Therefore they could not generate sufficient incomes to repay the loans from their own incomes generated from business with micro enterprises but were repaying from the borrowings of community and family networks. Ruth Pearson[13] added another dimension to the problem that the income generation by such enterprises is not uniform across classes and gender. Therefore the risks, the benefits and the implications of such credits vary enormously between these factors. Such business enterprises they stressed will not empower women.

With such evidences Bateman confirmed that the microfinance that in thirty years proved as—'the empty vessel'—even though it has risen to become one of the most publicised policy and programme interventions in the international development community[14] in the global financial sector (Milford Bateman, 2010)[15]. Therefore it is very evident that it will not lead to *sustainable economic and social development and it is not a proper policy intervention for sustainable poverty reduction* as has been assumed.

Barbara Harris White (2003) referring to such micro enterprises that are located in the informal, self-employment sector (80% of economy as she calls) argues that they are used as the instruments for capital accumulation along with the social institutions like religion, caste, space, class, gender relations.

She observed that based on such conditions of production for women, the present corporate economy could rest on the *guild system* (these are public institutions). In the system of the guilds workers were forced into the governance of the economy and the economy was controlled by a hierarchical system of social relations. For doing this, she states the *organizations of collective economic interests* may be created by the state and controlled by it for acceleration of capital accumulation.

The World Bank and Robert Putnam (1995, 2000)[16] in their proposition of social capital[17], explain as -*trust, cooperation* and *reciprocity* and loyalty that are assumed as imbibed features of women, work as the fabric for the structures of *voluntary associations and networks.* These social fabrics, *the authors argue, facilitate social and democratic participation for economic development and collective action* with their trustworthiness, reciprocity *and* mutual cooperation (Solow, 2000, Putnam, 1993, 2000). Coleman adds one more concept—the *intentions* as one of such *social capitals*. With this backdrop on the institutional arrangements for capital accumulation the following part of the study presents the SHGs as one such arrangement initiated by the state and shifted to an NGO in a free financial market. It is in this backdrop that the present study examines a decade of experience with SHGs and microfinance (that came later in the years after 2000) through a case study of the village and analysed the impact of these initiatives on female labour including those who have been experiencing displacement from farm employment as pointed out earlier.

II

The changes in the organizational, financial and operational structure of the SHGs under Government: The SHG programme was launched in the year 1999 in the village. The empirical data was collected by the scholar in the previous survey during January 2002 this has been used to look into the changes in the institutional, financial and operational structure of the of SHG programme.

Institutional Structure: The state launched the SHG programme under *"New Paradigm of Development" for the* stated objective under the banner of the eradication of poverty and empowerment of women in the village under study in 2001. They were started in the form of cooperative institutional structure. The state encouraged and expanded this programme by providing policy support with various incentives. The programme was brought under *priority sector lending*. This means that the banks are required to allocate 40 per cent of its total funds for extending credit to the SHGs. The incentives like free distribution of domestic cooking gas cylinders[18] (even today many women respondents stated that they joined the SHG for the sake of gas cylinders) were distributed. Gas became a necessity in the village in the context of development of business in land, enclosures and urbanization. The rural fuel became scarce. To start with 24 groups were mobilized with 10-15 members in each group. Each member contributed Rs 30 per month towards savings. These groups work with collateral security for getting bank loans.

Financial Structure: The World Bank Financed the *Velugu programme* at state level and the financial support for Development of Women and Children in Rural Areas (DWACRA) supported from the centre were started in 1999 (Vanamala, 2003).[19] The follow up of this programme is done in the changed name 'Revolving fund'. An amount of Rs 25000 per group was released to the state by the Government of India from 'Swarna Jayanthi Gram Swarojgar Yojna' by launching a new programme (SJSRGY). The funds were routed through the District Rural Development Agency (DRDA) and were intended to act as catalysts for the loan amount sanctioned by commercial banks. Thus there was a convergence of funds from the Government of India, State Government, commercial banks and savings of the SHG members.

Operational Structure: The National Agricultural Bank for

Reconstruction and Development (NABARD) lend loans to commercial banks at 7 per cent per annum, to lend this finances in turn to SHGs (Vanamala, 2001).[20] The rate of interest imposed by the commercial banks on SHG loans was 13.5 per cent per annum. During the year 2002 survey the SHGs in the village mobilized savings to the tune of Rs 2,03,530. Matching this amount an amount of Rs 25,000 grant was released by the Government of India. Based on these amounts of grants from the government, the banks released a loan amount of Rs 89,500.

An analysis of the evidence on operational data shows a contradiction to the policy statement on the ratio of savings and bank release. This ratio was prescribed as 1:4. Contrary to this ratio the savings amount shows four times to that of the bank loans. Another evidence from the operational structure is that the repayment of loans by the SHGs is not permitted by policy earlier than the stipulated period of 36 months. The evidences reveal that these policy conditions are more favourable for usury making than for poverty eradication or for empowerment of women (Vanamala, 2003). The source of finance shows that it is international finance that promoted the scheme with support of the state. The data shows that the total amount pooled from commercial banks, savings of the groups and subsidy together was a small amount for grounding any livelihood project. In this pooling, the field data (1A) shows that each member of the group could have access to Rs 7,993. These details are shown as follows in the year 2002 (Vanamala, 2003).

Table 1A: Savings of the SHG in the Village under Study during 1999 (estimated)

1 *Total no. of groups in the village.*	2 *Number of members in each group*	3 *Total members in the village (1x2)*	4 *Contribution of savings by each member PM in Rs*	5 *Total savings contributed per month (column 3x4=in Rs*	6 *Total savings contributed per annum 5x12 (months) = Rs*
24	15	360	30	10800	1,29,600

Source: Collected from the village SHGs

Table 1B: Details of Funds Worked Out to each Member of the SHG during 1999 in Rs.

1 *Savings of each group per annum 1,29600/24* *Rs*	2 *Revolving/ Matching grant released to each group* *Rs*	3 *Bank loan to each group* *Rs*	4 *Total corpus fund (columns 1+2+3) per group* *Rs*	5 *Total members in each group in number* *Rs*	6 *Per capita corpus funds available for investment to each member* *Rs*
5400	25, 000	89,500	119900	15	7993

Source: Data collected from Mandal office Patancheru.

Table 2A: Savings of the SHG in the Village under IKP Bank Linkage Programme during 2010

1 *Total no of groups in the village.*	2 *Number of members in each group*	3 *Total members in the village (1x2)*	4 *Contribution of saving by each member PM In Rs*	5 *Total saving contributed per month by all members 3x4=in Rs*	6 *contribution per annum* 5x12= Rs
65	15	975	100	97500	117,5,000

Source: Collected from village under study.

Table 2B: Savings Worked Out of the SHG in the Village Under Study during 2010

1 *Savings of each SHG per annum 11,75,000/65*	2 *Revolving/ Matching Grant released to each group Rs*	3 *Bank loan to each group in the first bank linkage*	4 *Total corpus fund 1+2+3 in Rs*	5 *Total members In each group number*	6 *Per capita corpus funds available for investment to each member.*
18,077	Nil	50,000 (1st linkage)	68,000	15	4533

Source: Collected from village under study.[21]

A comparison of the financial and physical data in the years 1999 (Tables 1A,1B) and 2009-10 (2A, 2B) shows that although the number of SHGs increased (with above mentioned efforts of the state) from 24 to 65 and the membership and savings by each member has gone up from Rs 30 per month per person to Rs 100. The total corpus fund decreased from Rs 1,19,900 to Rs 68,000 and per head funds decreased from Rs 7,993 to Rs 4,533 under IKP programmes. The funds from SGSY are diverted for the community development programme which further reduced the funds under IKP borrowings. This further confirms that any scheme could hardly be grounded with that amount hence loans are used for consumption purposes. The borrowers continue to depend on loans. Assets for livelihood makes them independent.

The following field data provides further evidence on this argument. Although the policy stipulates that the SHG loans are not meant for consumption purposes but meant only for creation of livelihood assets. Contary to this hardly any amount is used for the purpose of asset building. The empirical evidence shows that out of the 77sample SHG members 58 per cent have diverted their funds from asset creation (during 2002). The remaining 42 per cent of them have invested in their already running enterprises which do not create an additional employment.

It is also revealing that the banks have preferred lending to family-based units. The date shows it is as high as 62 per cent of total lending. The new individual-based female-headed units have an insignificant share in the total SHG loan amount. This resulted in the 94 per cent of SHG members who did not ground independent units that are potentially could increase new employment and income. (Vanamala, 2003). This evidence clearly indicates that the state is indifferent to violation of its stipulated policy prescriptions. The state also did not show any commitment to attend its own promises in critical needs of the SHG members.

The evidence in 1999 shows that the problem of illiteracy among the SHG leaders (during 2002) was as high as 48 percent. Although the policy has categorically identified that *the sustainable development is possible only with development of education and skills among the SHG members.* The data shows there have been no efforts whatsoever on behalf of the government for promotion of literacy and skills among them.

On the social mobility the observation shows that although frictions and tensions were found in the relationship of husband and wife permitting the wife to go to SHG meetings some positive trends like (Vanamala, 2003) more than 63 per cent of women were attending the meetings and this has become a strong social force against domestic violence. This was an unintended social outcome.

From here the SHG movement has taken a turn when the groups that were started by the government have been shifted to the Society for Elimination of Rural Poverty (SERP), launched by an NGO. This new programme for SHG is called the 'Integrated programme' working under the project of Indira Kranthi Patham (IKP). It sets its functions as follows.

As has been mentioned earlier the original source of finances for the SHG are from the World Bank financed under Velugu programme, which was started in 1992 and another programme under the DWACRA programme of the Central Government mentioned above were brought under the Society for Elimination of Rural Poverty (SERP)[22] from 2004-05. The SERP is an *autonomous* registered *society.*[23] The IKP is only a *facilitating organization at the project level*. The employment expansion under it is indirect through SHGs. The staff recruited for IKP is under a specific HR Policy (Government of AP)[24] specially enacted for it. It clearly explains that the state is under pressure of the World Bank for implementation of the programme for SHGs.

The access to loans in IKP is with the bank linkage programmes which are *regular and cumulative*. Apart from the bank linkage finances the SERP also provides loans from the Community Investment Fund (CIF)[25] which come from the SGSY scheme. The funds from SGSY are meant for the poor communities to improve their livelihoods by investing in micro enterprises proposed and implemented by the community (SHGs/VOs/Mandals, Samakhyas (MS) and other common interest groups). The source and the route of IKP funds flow as follows.

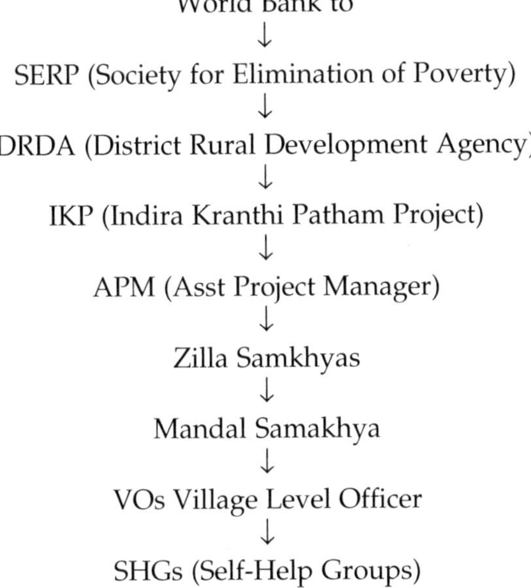

The IKP expanded its resources from higher to higher level for doing its financial business under so called "integrated programme" with expanded functions of IKP. This expanded business of IKP has been reducing the role of the state to a minimal and to that of a facilitator. The expanded institutional (during 2002) structure of IKP is as follows.

Changes in the Structure of SHG: After the shift of SHG from government to IKP, their structure was enlarged and expanded from cooperative into a federal form in the open financial market. To accelerate the financial business the cluster organizational structure is adopted. Every 30 SHGs of a village form one VO. At village level 15 to 50 SHGs constitute cluster taking one or two members from each cluster federations are formed. From each federation one or two members are drawn to form a Samakhya. This is the apex body at the Mandal level. From each Mandal Samahkhya one or two are drawn to form a Zilla Samkhya. The SHGs which were informal groups in the earlier structure are now made formal by registering under different private financial institutions. The SHGs from the village are registered under the Andhra Pradesh Mahila Abhivruddi Society (APMAS) and also under Mutually Aided Cooperative Societies. The other changes initiated in lending systems were for instance the banks under bank linkage programme the loans were made cumulative. Most striking rule resting change was that IKP introduced the Internal Lending System (lending among the group members) to expand the financial business. The expansion of IKP is reflected in the following data.

The state-wide details of SHGs show that there are 1,11,02,494 members in 9,94,595 SHGs exclusively for women. A total of 38,550 village organizations (VOs), 1098 Mandal Samakhyas(MSs) and 22 Zilla Samakhyas have come into existence in 22 districts. As on July 2011 the total savings and corpus fund of SHGs members are Rs 3383.10 crores and Rs 5070.51 crores respectively. From inception of the bank linkage programmes till 2011, the bank loans stood at Rs 7092.71 crores (see Table 3).

Table 3. Coverage under the Bank Linkage Programme

Parameters	*2004-05*	*2005-06*	*2006-07*	*2007-08*	*2008-09*	*2009-10*	*2010-11*
Coverage of groups	261254	288711	366489	431515	483601	413625	389444
Amount of loan (Rs crores)	1017.70	2001.40	3063.87	5882.79	6684.07	6501.35	7092.71
No of branches	3853	3853	3950	4000	4150	4274	4286
Per group finance (Rs)	38954	69322	83601	136329	137498	157180	182123
Groups per branch	68	75	93	108	118	97	91

Source:http//www.rd.ap.gov.in/ikpnew.htm 8-26-2011

The data in Table (3) shows that coverage of groups increased from Rs 2,612,54 in 2004 to Rs 389444 in 2011. The amount of loan increased from Rs 1,017.70 to Rs 7,092.71 during this period. The per-group finance has grown from Rs 38,954 to Rs 1,82,123. The other programmes taken up by IKP are as follows.

Total Financial Inclusion (TFI): This is yet another programme with a higher level of allotment of loan funds. The APM says the success of this financial programme depends on the training awareness and management skills at unit level. Under the TFI Rs 5,00,000 will be sanctioned to an individual woman borrower under the third linkage of bank. These loans do not need any security or any asset holding by the borrower. Out of the TFI amount 50 per cent of it is meant for repayment of bad debts. From the remaining 50 per cent 25 per cent is meant for social expenditure and the remaining 25 per cent per cent of loan amount borrowed needs to be invested on micro enterprise that generates income. This entire amount is a loan from the bank with 14 per cent of interest. The repayment would be in 60 Equal Instalments (EMIs). This works out to Rs 3,50,000 interest in a five-year period. The loan amount plus interest works out to Rs 8,50,000. This amount to be repaid works out to almost double the amount borrowed. The promotion of such financial institutions in the state is a clear case of wide expansion of business in finance. The above mentioned programmes are earmarked for different requirements of the borrower. This clearly explains that the vulnerability of the needy has been encashed by the financial institution to expand its business. This is where the effect and the consequences of the programme are different for different borrower.

Periodical Increase in Savings of the SHGs: The field data shows the following savings of the group that are meant for internal lending (within group members) have been expanding. The project officer says that these savings have risen up to one lakh with each group.

The pass books issued by the bank to SHGs show the rate of interest they charge. Based on this data and with the help of the interview with the APM a tentative amount of the interest on loans are worked out in the following estimates.[26]

The financial institution/bank can earn an amount of Rs 2,530 as interest on the savings of each SHG for the first year (see Table 2B for annual savings per group 18077) at the rate of 14 per cent of simple interest per annum. For 18 months this amount works out to Rs 3,795. This interest will not be credited to the group's account. This is unaccounted for members and belongs totally to the bank. At the end of eighteen months the SHG becomes eligible for the first loan. The loan sanctioned after 18 months is Rs 50,000 to each group. The bank earns an additional amount of Rs 7,000 interest a year on this loan. At the end of the fourth year (in a period of 24 months the loan of 50,000 has to be cleared). The total interest by this time works out to another Rs 7,000. This together comes to Rs 2530+7000+ 7000= Rs 16,530 per group. This is the minimum amount earned by the financial institution/bank in two year's time. Or for the first loan amount the total (65) groups in the village lose Rs 10, 74,550. This is the minimum amount a bank earns in two years on all groups in a year. The amounts for the second and the third loans is higher and the interest amount would also go up.

The banks play a trick in the collection of interest. They collect interest after clearance of the principal loan amount. Total interest amount to be repaid by members is never informed to the members. It is observed that there is a column in the pass book of SHG to enter the rate of interest. This has been left blank by the institutions/banks. When the SHG members questioned it, they stated, 'that will be worked out after repayment of the principal amount'. This raises doubts that; will they reduce the amount paid in installments or will they charge a flat rate on the total amount till the loan is cleared? The members are not informed of the total amount of interest, the number of instalments for repayment of interest. This takes care of the deferred loan payments. If some member is in dire need of a higher amount, than what she gets as a member, she can borrow it internally from other members of the group who are not in need immediately. For this money the member has to bear an additional 24 per cent of interest. The rules for these informal loans are not prepared for regularization of loan).

Against these practices in the federated institutions like IKP the loans disbursed from DRDA shows a clear picture of the interest rate charged (14%), number of instalments for repayment of loan (20), amount of each instalment is clearly mentioned in the pass books.

There are additional collections by federated institutions like—a fee of Rs 100 is to be paid by each member every year to be a member of the federation. An additional amount of Rs 10 is to be paid every month to the Village Gram Panchayat to be a member in the VO.

By policy, the repayment worked out is 60 EMIs. For this the interest on loan 3,50,000 with simple interests in 60 instalments (five-year period) comes to 8,50,000. This amount is almost double the amount borrowed by a SHG member. The promotion of such financial institutions in the state is a clear case of facilitation for appropriation of incomes of rural vulnerable sections. The entire structure of the SHG and credit policy vividly explain that the commercial banks and private financial institutions are depleting the rural meagre subsistence income of the households.[27]

The Community Investment Funds: From the funds of the rural development head the CIF is created. The APM stated that out of the total budget of the IKP project, CIF is the most important fund that determines the level of employment for the poor. This fund acts as a catalyst in capital formation at the levels of SHG, VO and Mandal Samakhya (MS) and offers great leverage for raising bank loans. The CIF fund, the APM stated, is used broadly for three activities of IKP, one, income generation activities, two, development of productive infrastructure and three, for the development of social activities. Now the financial institutions are negotiating for change of the CIF to infrastructure development and merge SHG under it in the IKP programmes. This change would further help in enhancing the financial business.

Under micro plan based intervention strategy of the state, CIF is a loan from Mandal Samakhya (MS) to Village Office (VO) to SHGs for implementing the micro plan of the SHGs collective and for food security. District Project Manager Unit (DPMU) releases the CIF to MSs in instalments up to their Mandal entitlement. This change in the forms of funds release is a clear case of subordinating the state power to that of private financial institution and in the name of food security financial business for consumption gets expanded.

Swarna Jayanthi Swarojgar Yojana (SGSY): This was a credit-cum subsidy programme with 75:25 shared funds by the centre and state. The 'National Network Enabling Self-Help Movement' (NN-ABLE) is an NGO that expressed the following views on the expected functioning of SHG. The NGO stated that credit is the critical component and subsidy is only an enabling element. The objective of the programme was to strengthen the SHG and a large number of micro enterprises in the rural areas. Operation of the programme is done by an NGO. The programme focuses on the vulnerable sections like SCs, STs and women. The programme in practice permits only one member from a family in a group although the scheme is planned to assist to a group. He added that this scheme is expected to generate Rs 2,000 additional income per Swarojgar per month. The group programmes are expected to generate Rs 11,000 per month per group. Since its inception in 1999 to December 2008-09, the programme assisted 35.7 lakh SHGs with an assistance of Rs 1.24 Cr in establishing their own micro-enterprises. The bank credit mobilized was Rs 19,017 cores; total subsidy provided was Rs 9,318 crores. The following Table (4) shows the percentage of utilization of these funds.

Table 4. Percentage of Utilization of SGSY Funds

Year	*Subsidy*	*Revolving fund*	*Infrastructure development*	*Training capacity building*
1999-00	36.79	5.06	22.16	4.65
2000-01	52.67	6.73	24.45	4.32
2000-02	86.16	8.79	15.79	4.97
2000-03	65.78	12.58	14.79	4.47
2000-04	68.37	15.14	14.47	4.91
2000-05	66.52	10.79	14.1	5.9
2000-06	67.59	11.08	13.3	6.31
2000-07	68.18	9.86	12.99	7.26
2000-08	65.57	9.52	15.98	9.76
2000-09	76.42	13.87	14.23	9.24
Total	65.4	10.34	16.23	6.18

Source: Government of India, (GoI), 2009

The data in Table 4 shows that the subsidy utilized was more than 65 per cent of targeted amount and revolving fund utilized was more than 10 per cent of target amount. Based on this data the financial pressure groups argued for a change of these allocations. They want to double the allocations on infrastructure, training by shifting them from the allocation from Rojgar schemes. The government constituted an expert committee for the evaluation of the SGSY programme under Radhakrishna as chairman (known as Radha Krishna Committee). This committee also involved the institutions such as RBI, NIRD, BIRD, NIBM, NIPFP. The committee expressed the following views on the SGSY structure and functioning.

It is stated that this programme SGSY has never taken-off as it encountered numerous implementation problems[28] such as- adverse impact of SGSY subsidy limits the expansion of bank credit. The committee added that loans are raised only for the sake of subsidy amount. The subsidy is so low that it conditioned the credit subsidy ratio to be at much lower than the target ratio of 3:1 (GoI, 2009) (see Table 4). Experts held that the programme resulted in less than planned investment per Swarozgar. It was also expressed that SCs and STs got excluded from the financial assistance and the SGSY covered only one per cent of the relevant households. It was also alleged that malpractice was noticed in the coverage and in maintenance of assets. The institutions involved in assessment of the programme maintained that the rich have benefited more from SGSY than the poor particularly the SCs and STs. Based on these views of the expert group, the financial pressure groups worked-out for a change of financial and implementation structures of SGSY. The new structure is formulated with change of ratio of scheme subsidy and capital subsidy. The share of capital subsidy is doubled and interest subsidy was introduced. The financial pressure groups worked for individualist schemes to SHG members in the place of group schemes of SGSY. There was pressure from financial institution for reduction of state intervention along with scheme subsidy. Eventually the SGSY programme was redesigned under

National Rural Livelihood Mission (NRLM)[29] with change of role of the state from the budget provider to that of facilitator (Tanka Ajay, et al., 2008).[30] Thus the private financial supremacy over state has been clearly established. The state in AP started a modified programme in the name of ***Pavala Vaddi*** since 2004 in the place of the SGSY programme. (see the working of the Pavala Vaddi programme in case studies). After financial supremacy has been established over the state, restructuring in tune with the financial reforms as part of restructured globalization and privatization during this period. This paved the way to instil the ***for-profit*** financial institutions in the financial market. (see changes in the financial market in Annexure 1 and II). Following these changes in the financial market the following microfinance companies entered the village under study for their business.

Working of Microfinance Company: Finance companies like L&T, SKS, Spandana, Basix and Sahara are found lending microfinance in the village. The Micro Finance Institutions create separate SHGs. They put five members in a group based on the same business the members intend to do. Then the MFI staff collect the copies of immobile property ownership papers like a house. For residence proof, the copies of electricity bills and ration cards from all five members of the group. Agreement papers duly signed by members for collateral security are obtained. After completion of this process the loan is sanctioned.

The micro finance institutions have adopted different loan recovery systems. MFI like SKS and Asmitha recover loans on a weekly basis while institutions like Spandana, Bsix and Sahara recover it every month. If anybody fails in payment of any instalment, the other members are held responsible. Internally they charge interest to any SHG member who cannot pay on time. Under each of the above MFIs there are 10 to 30 groups in the village. The borrower says that MFI charge 24 per cent of interest on the loans borrowed. The companies collect the transaction costs like Rs 20 per cent of the loan amount towards service charges, collect 10 per cent of loan towards operating cost, another 10 per cent for insurance (The insurance is a misnomer). This is charged for the loan insurance not for the insurance of the borrower. Two to five per cent of loan is collected towards profits for the company. The costs work out to more than 69 per cent which are spread into Equal Monthly/ Weekly payments. (author died notes). The problems with such growth of MFI have been alerted by Y.V. Reddy, former governor, RBI. He held that "the MFI are growing too rapidly and making too much profit for comfort". He further cautioned the policy makers that in the face of the consequent build-up of liquidity, elevated asset prices and soaring consumer indebtedness seems to be leading to the dark future.[31] He cautioned about the financial business institutions and said that they borrow money from International Financial Institutions, and also from the banks in the country at a lower rate of interest and lend to SHGs at a higher rate of interest. He observed that they maintained no upper limit for charging the rate of interest for lending the loan amounts and there is no regulation to limit the rate of interest by these institutions. He added that the policy is indifferent on lending by multiple institutions to the same borrower and that too without the specified purpose of loan.

At present the growth of microfinance institutions in the state of Andhra Pradesh is very rapid. There are 47 registered microfinance institutions along with several other institutions which are not registered. These microfinance institutions formed into "The Microfinance Institutional Net Work" with an "Information Bureau". This rapid growth and pattern of networking and farming into information bureau suggests that these institutions compete for monopoly power in the financial market, which will eventually follow other powers. The monopolies can lead to reckless speculation and crisis in the economy. There was massive protest in the civil society against this crisis in AP. This issue was referred to 'The Malegam Committeee'. The committee was insensitive to the problems of SHG and gave a judgment in support of the financial institutions allowing 24 per cent rate of interest to be charged[11] on loans borrowed by SHG, along with other transaction costs. However, a brake was applied to this reckless business by the state government that promulgated 'The Andhra Pradesh Microfinance Ordinance' on October 15, 2010 against MFIs using coercive recollection practices and charging usurious interest rates. The Ordinance ordered MFIs to register with the state government and specified the power for suo-moto to shut down MFI activity. A number of NBFCs have been affected by this ordinance, including heavyweights like SKS Microfinance. The following case studies on all types of SHGs in the village will provide a deeper insight into this model of development.

The Case Studies of SHG members **on the Pavala Vaddi Scheme**

Name of the Paval Vaddi **Rojgari: Gadde Kamalamma**

Particulars of Household Members of Rojgari

S. No.	*Members*	*Occupation*	*Earnings Rs PM*
1	Rojgari	Vege	3069
2	1st son	Pla.business	4000
3	2nd son	Saharabank	5000
4	Daughter-in-law	Housewife	-
5	Daughter-in-law	Housewife	-
6	3rd son	Student	-

Husband: The late G. Pandu expired 20 years ago.
Caste: Madiga
Assets: Nil
Name of the micro enterprise: Vegetable vending.
EMI: Rs 1,640@0.25% interest

Microenterprise in Marketing of the Vegetables

Vegetable	*Sales in kgs per week*	*Purchases per week in Rs*	*Sales in Rs per week*	*Turnover per week Rs*
Tomato	92 @Rs 7 per kg	600	644	44
Cauliflower	80	600	840	240
Chilli	70	1120	1400	280
Onions	100	800	1000	200
Drumsticks	50 number	120	125	05
Total	————	3240	4009	769

Collected from the Respondent

The data on this rojgari shows that Vadde Kamalamma, a vegetable vendor has been engaged in this activity for the last 20 years. The loan availed of is not for livelihood activity but for other contingent expenditure of household. She also has better household conditions as her two sons work. One does business another is employed in a bank and draws Rs 5,000 per month. This case shows that the bank has come forward to lend to this woman taking into account her and her son's repayment capacity and long experience in business. The credit has been utilized as a means of survival rather than to enhance the growth of employment.

She is paying Rs 1,640 per month for the loan she has raised.

Her monthly earnings as per the table above worked out to Rs 3,076 per month, saving an amount of Rs 1,436. This amount is less than the stipulated earning of Rs 2,000 per month by the policy

CASE-2 K. Pentamma
Husband: Pentiah
Caste: Madiga
Assets: Nil
Name of the micro enterprise: fruits business.
EMI: Rs 1,040 per month.
Cumulative loan amounts raised by Rojgari in Rs

1st loan	2nd loan	3rd loan
5,000	10,000	15,000

Details of family members

Name	*Age*	*Occupation*
Pentamma rojgari	50	Fruit business
Pentiah husband	56	Fruit business
Narsimha son	35	Fruit business
Lakshimi daughter	27	Fruit business
Prasad (grandson)	4	-
Shivakumar (grandson)	2	-

Source: Collected from rojgar respondent.

Fruit	*Purchase@Rs per Kg*	*Sell@Rs per Kg*	*Per day sales in Kgs*	*Benefit Rs per day*
Grapes	40	60	50	100
Sapota	20	40	50	100
Total			100	200

Source: Collected from rojgari

K. Pentamma has been engaged in the fruit business for the last 20 years. Four members in the family are employed on this. The earnings work out to Rs 50 per day per person. This is much less than the daily market wages in the village. It is also observed that all activities do not carry the same prestige in the village social system. The nature of activity that they do is based on the caste and occupational background of the family. She is not interested in the expansion of business. The amount she borrowed in the programme is used for household expenditure.

Case Study of the Village SHGs under IKP: A sample of 91 female respondents has been drawn for the study. A stratification of a cross section of social groups and occupations are used to draw this sample. The social groups drawn are, three respondents from the scheduled tribes (STs), 25 from the scheduled castes (SCs), 44 from the backward castes (BCs) and 19 respondents from the forward castes (OCs) (Q.!.1). The age particulars of the respondents are, 12 per cent of them are under 25 years, others are between 26 to 45 years. Among the members 18 per cent are between 46 to 60 years. The educational particulars of these respondents indicate that 56 per cent of them are illiterates and near illiterates (primary). Nine per cent completed upper primary education; about 30 per cent have completed secondary educational levels. Those who have done intermediate education constituted a mere six percent. Among the social groups all STs are in the illiteracy category 92 per cent from SCs, 91 per cent from BCs and about 90 per cent from OCs fall in this category. In the categories that completed primary and upper primary, the OCs constitute more than 21 percent, BCs form 9 per cent and SCs 8 percent. This data shows that even though most of these SHG members have been in this organization for a minimum period of 19 years, their illiteracy has not come down. The occupational stratification of the sample members is as follows.

Q.No. 1.4. Main Occupations of the SHG Respondents

Main occupation			*Caste*		
	ST	*SC*	*BC*	*OC*	*Total*
Own Agriculture	0	2	0	0	2
	0.0	8.0	0.0	0.0	2.2
Housewife	1	11	16	7	35
	33.3	44.0	36.4	36.8	38.5
Government Employee	1	2	0	1	4
	33.3	8.0	0.0	5.3	4.4
Industrial Contract Worker	0	2	3	1	6
	0.0	8.0	6.8	5.3	6.6
Unskilled business	0	1	8	3	12
	0.0	4.0	18.2	15.8	13.2
Tailor	0	3	7	5	15
	0.0	12.0	15.9	26.3	16.5
Sari Rolling	0	0	1	1	2
	0.0	0.0	2.3	5.3	2.2
Construction Worker	1	3	7	0	11
	33.3	12.0	15.9	0.0	12.1
Non-agricultural labour	0	0	1	1	2
	0.0	0.0	2.3	5.3	2.2
Agriculture labour	0	1	0	0	1
	0.0	4.0	0.0	0.0	1.1
Dhobi	0	0	1	0	1
	0.0	0.0	2.3	0.0	1.1
Total	3	25	44	19	91
	100.0	100.0	100.0	100.0	100.0

The above table shows that 39 per cent of the sample respondents are housekeepers. When this data is projected, it covers the occupational conditions of the total 1,042 members from the sample groups (of 91) out of these members. These SHG women never invested their borrowings on enterprise.

The analysis of the nature of occupations of these women shows that sample respondents are mainly in 10 types of occupations. Four per cent are in the government employment in Gram Panchayat as contract workers whose payments run between Rs 2,000-5,000 per month, about seven per cent of them are industrial contract workers. Nineteen per cent of women are engaged in petty self-employed business like tailoring and sari rolling. The other occupations that engaged these women are labour or petty family firms. The SHG programme has not helped the members to get decent work.

The analysis of the earnings of these workers shows that most of them earn very meagre incomes. These informal self-employment business units are carried on in the residence as they cannot afford to run them in rented shops outside the residences (case studies of the microenterprise are taken up in the later part of the study). But the earnings from all these activities are uncertain and low as there are hardly any avenues which could be accessed for upgradation of skills in this fast changing market. This explains the vulnerability and poor conditions of these women in the village under study which have not been addressed by SHG programme. The conditions of SHG women working on micro enterprises and conditions of labour are not very different.

The analyses of the occupations of the female respondents across the social group's shows 33 per cent of STs, 44 per cent of SCs, 36 per cent of BCs and 37 per cent of OCs are housewives. This is followed by the business in tailoring picked up through informal learning. This is followed by petty business. The petty business is a family occupation, which does not allow women to exercise independence over earnings. Such vulnerable conditions have not been improved by the SHG programme.

The sample data shows that 13 per cent of the families have rented out a portion of their house for their livelihood. Another 16 per cent have retained a small land holding which is mostly kept fallow and households joined the labour market. As these holdings can't sustain a family of two adults and two children from its production. This data clearly explains that the respondents continue to be poor and the loans from SHG did not make any significant difference.

The occupations of the husbands of these women SHG members are also not different from their spouses. The permanent workers in the industries constitute only two per cent who have regular incomes. About 98 per cent husbands of the sample respondents do not have occupations which get them regular income. Out of them 13 per cent and 32 per cent are contract workers in government (Gram Panchayat) and in industries, 19 per cent of them are engaged in petty rural business. About seven per cent are engaged in new technical activities like welding, electrical jobs, driving and some are engaged in petty real estate work. The remaining seven per cent are in the labour market. This evidence confirms further that in the last 20 years of the SHG scheme the poverty of the households remained, almost at the same level.

The data on the repayment of the loan instalments reveal promptness and almost 95 per cent of the borrowers repay them regularly. However it is observed that the repayments are not from the earnings of the borrowers but mostly from the husband's earnings.

The details on the purpose of spending the loan amounts reveal that only 30 per cent of the respondents spent on purchase of livelihood assets and the remaining of 70 per cent spent on daily needs. Out of those that purchased assets, 17 per cent of them stated that they invested on their business that is already in the market, three per cent of them invested in agriculture and one per cent each purchased buffaloes and other employable assets. Eleven per cent of them stated that they spent loans on multiple needs like medical care, children's education, clearance of earlier debt and spent on marriages. The data on the loan amount spent shows that except two per cent who purchased buffaloes and other assets, 98 per cent spent it without generating any new employment. The expenditure on minimum needs is more than the previous days on account of changes in the medical systems. Out of those who spent on minimum needs, 19 per cent mentioned that the loan was used for clearance of earlier debts, eight per cent of them mentioned that they used it for household expenditure, 11 per cent said it was used on health care, 3.3 per cent stated that they spent it for marriage, 10 per cent used it for children's education and yet another 10 per cent used it for extension of their living house. Two per cent of them used the amount for purchase of gold. As high as 15 per cent stated that they do not know how it is spent by their husbands indicating patriarchic culture.

The entire structure of the SHG is strategically built on social capital. For instance, to a question—how do you manage the repayment of the loan (Q.No. 45) four types of answers were given by the respondents. A majority of them constituting 79 per cent stated that they meet repayment of loans from their husband's or **from the earnings of the family members**. Generally 21 per cent of them fail to pay in time. In such cases the collateral payment is done by other members of the group. The attributes of social capital like ***trustworthiness*** and the ***reciprocity*** are tapped to enhance the value of capital (see Q.No. 45).

At the village level the organizations of SHG are facing several problems. The data elicited by asking a question that whether they want to become a leader (Q.No. 10), more than 82 per cent of them answered no. Among those who said no have specified the following reasons, 43 per cent of them said they are not interested because of the probable interpersonal problems that crop up with members, about 19 per cent said they are busy with domestic work or business. About 17 per cent of them said they cannot be leaders as they are illiterates.

Further probing by attending the monthly meetings of the SHGs it is learnt that the problem of illiteracy is found to be a very serious obstruction for carrying forward the operations of such a programme. No single member of SHG women either hold or operate the bank account. This activity is done only by the SHG leaders. The accounts keeping is done by SHG members by paying a monthly salary from personal sources to SHG educated women. This has led to rupture in the interpersonal relations. At a meeting attended by the research team it is observed that the accountant demanded enhancement of her salary against that she has been maintaining accounts of

100 members and is finding it difficult and over burdened. In this deliberation the accountant used unparliamentary language against SHG members. This particular behaviour of the accountant appears that the capital has won control and devided the community life in the village. The further probe into the problems of illiteracy has thrown up new issues.

The illiteracy worked as a boon to the financial institutions to prey on it like "vultures". The programme introduced various informal operations that extract money from the members. The SHG members who come late to the meetings were fined Rs 10 as penalty. For such a collection no accounts are maintained. Such informal extraction practices are also observed while attending the Mandal level meetings by the leaders. Each time money is collected by the group leader for this purpose. The money collected is said to be meeting the expenditure of leaders on transport and expenditure on items like food of the federation members, meeting the lunch expenditure for federation members is made mandatory for SHG members. These expenses are unaccounted. The additional amount collected for such expenses on leaders of SHG is not accounted for. This causes a rupture in relations between leaders and members of SHGs. The illiteracy helps the manipulators to dupe the SHG members.

Despite every year's auditing of the accounts of the groups by the concerned authorities, the management sends the *outstanding dues of* the groups of previous years. The dues get multiplied. The observation reveals that when a leader exits from the leadership, the management takes advantage of this, and strategically mismanages the group accounts. This leads to collection of money from such groups again. This strategy helps to divide the members into insiders (leaders are insiders to capital) and outsiders (SHG) and also to make easy profits. Owing to illiteracy the members shy away from knowing the actual details about the schemes.

The SHG women are unaware of the objectives of the programme. This situation triggers the profit earning institutions to mislead women. In this connection an experience is worth recalling. A respondent belonging to the Scheduled Caste community asked the researcher which organization she represented, when replied from the 'government', she immediately said, "If it is government, it is always ***good*** to believe as it helps us". This is the reputation earned by the welfare state under constitutional mandatory for the last 60 years of its administration, particularly in respect of the Scheduled Castes. To know further about the ill-informed SHG members, it is attempted to find out the expected role of the SHG leaders. The respondents stated, it is collection of money from the group members (Q.No. 9, 17 percent), attending and coordinating the meetings of the SHGs (6 percent, 13 percent). From these responses it is clear that the SHG members think the functions of the leaders are limited to carry out the business in finance.

The SHG is generally considered as a voluntary social force. From this one expects that the leaders feel responsible to demand justice to empower their members. The leaders have become free clerical staff to the financial capital. The role, informal practices adopted and functions done or got done for free of cost by the SHG leaders and members explain that these practices of exploitation by the capital are institutionalized for capital accumulation.

The social transition include a change in patriarchic attitudes is significant. The field observations show that those husbands of SHG members who objected for their spouses going to SHG meetings during the 1990s have changed and encourage them by 2010, as 100 per cent respondents said that their husbands encouraged their participation in SHG activities.

One more significant change in this sphers is the patriarchic relations between mother-in-law and daughter-in-law also changed. The daughter-in-law being better exposed, she is sent to SHG meetings as a priority. During this time the mother-in-law takes care of domestic work and children. It is also observed that this change in attitude is a key for the sustenance of the women in the SHG and SHG programme. Generally women being able to move out of the house into public space is interpreted as empowerment, although it is the deteriorating economic conditions that forced them to change. The following data on the series of loans availed by the SHGs further reinforced the argument that there is deterioration in economic conditions of these households.

The data on the number of loans availed of by each member in her entire membership time is elicited'. Out of 91 sample respondents, those who availed of single loans constitute 25 (Q.No. 26). Those who availed of two loans constitute 23 (two members dropped out), those who availed of three loans constitute 29 (six joined) and those who availed of four loans constitute 19. This shows the trend of drop out from the cumulative loan system (see Q. no. 26). Those who availed of the fifth to eighth loan is a single respondent. This explains that there is a high dropout rate from the fourth loan onwards. It seems a renewal into the programme of the drop outs has taken place in the third loan. After the fourth loan a heavy dropout is seen.

Q.No. 26. Number of Sample Respondents Availed Cumulative Loans

Social group	*1*	*2*	*3*	*4*	*5*	*6*	*7*	*8*	*Total*
ST	1	2	0	0	0	0	0	0	3
	33.3	66.7	0.0	0.0	0.0	0.0	0.0	0.0	100.0
SC	5	6	7	6	0	0	1	0	25
	20.0	24.0	28.0	24.0	0.0	0.0	4.0	0.0	100.0
BC	12	10	14	6	1	0	0	1	44
	27.3	22.7	31.8	13.6	2.3	0.0	0.0	2.3	100.0
OC	5	3	5	5	0	1	0	0	19
	26.3	15.8	26.3	26.3	0.0	5.3	0.0	0.0	100.0
Total	23	21	26	17	1	1	1	1	91
	25.3	23.1	28.6	18.7	1.1	1.1	1.1	1.1	100.0

Q.No. 26. Number of Sample Respondents Availed Cumulative Loans (number of loans)

Social group	*1*	*2*	*3*	*4*	*5*	*6*	*7*	*8*	*Total*
ST	1	2	0	0	0	0	0	0	3
SC	5	6	7	6	0	0	1	0	25
BC	12	10	14	6	1	0	0	1	44
OC	5	3	5	5	0	1	0	0	19
Total	23	21	26	17	1	1	1	1	91

Source: Field Study

Q.No.27. First Loan Availed-Slab-wise by the Sample Members

Social group	*Less than Rs 3,500 %*	*Rs 3500-4,500*	*Rs 4500-5,500*	*Above Rs 5,500*	*Total*
ST	1	1	0	1 %	3
SC	9	0	3	13	25
BC	17	1	15	11	44
OC10	1	4	4	19	
Total	37 (40.65)	3	22	29 (31.86)	91

The analysis of the first loan and the loan slab shows that about 41 per cent of the members are in the loan slab of less than Rs 3,500, more than 21 per cent availed of it from the loan slab of Rs 4,500-5,500. This is followed by about 32 per cent of members who availed of the loan from the highest loan slab of Rs 5500 and above. This explains that there is a demand pattern that shows a high demand for low amounts (perhaps from petty activity sections) followed by high demand for high amounts (from commercial activity sections). The demand in the middle level slab shows a moderate demand (this could be from the farming section). This explains a clear inequality in availing of the loan amount. With this socio-economic background of SHG members the following part presents case studies on microenterprises set by SHG members for livelihood earnings.

III

Case Studies of SHG Members under Micro Enterprises

The SHG members are not aware of policy objectives that the credit is meant for setting up of micro enterprises. Recently the Ministry of National Council for Skill Development advised the Rural Development Ministry to build skills among the member of 'The National Rural Employment Guarantee Scheme (NREGS)'.[12] So far no structure is developed to train the SHG members to ground any enterprise. Members are left on their own to set up the micro enterprises. The policy on micro-enterprises expects SHGs to promote and produce without any encumbrances of finance and infrastructural facilities. The following secondary data explains the huge contributions from these enterprises countrywide.

According to the 2006-07 medium and small Micro-enterprises (MSME) census, 94 per cent of them are the unregistered units and generated employment for 594.6 lakh persons which works out 85 per cent of the total employment of that sector.[13] The share of the MSME sector in the country's industrial output stood at about 45 per cent in 2008-09. Exports by MSME amounted to Rs 2,02,017 crores in 2007-08 contributing to about 16 per cent of total exports. For the reason of nature of non-encumbrance and high productivity the microenterprises are encouraged. The following case studies reinforce this argument further.

Case 1: N. Padma

Caste: Gouda (economically rising class, caste occupation of male is liquor business)

Age: 34 years

Education: Studied up to the seventh class.

Name of the enterprises: Wet grinder, peaco and tailoring (two enterprises were set together).

Husband's occupation: A labour contractor, a commission agent of the industries.

Husband owns no arable land:

Availed loan of Rs 70,000 @ 24% per annum

Husband/respondent owns a three- room slab house.

Husband's contribution for the enterprise is in terms of repairs of the grinder and sewing machines. He learnt these skills from the industries to which he supplies the labour. He purchases the raw material required for the enterprise.

On her own house. The front hall is used for the business.

She had no formal training, she learnt tailoring from her mother.

Only son who is studying. She underwent a histrectomy operation at the age of 25.

It is observed by the researchers that this village is low lying, the let-outs from surrounding industries flow into it. Therefore in every on an average one person suffers from ailments.

SHG member: For ten years she was a member of the Velugu programme and continued into IKP. The expenditure and income details of her enterprises are as follows.

Enterprise	*Total expenditure on raw material in week*	*Earnings in week on wet grinder*	*Earnings in week on tailoring*	*Total savings in a week*
Wet grinder				
2HP motor	Rs 70	Rs 350	—	Rs 280
sewing machine	Rs 70	Rs 140	Rs 70	Rs 70

Interest rate worked out = Rs 140 PM @24% per annum on Rs 70,000 loan

Total income per month 350X4= Rs 1,400 PM on

both the activities. Net Savings after deduction of interest to be paid PM=1400-140= Rs 1,260 PM net earnings after deduction of interest

The opportunity costs of the rent on house for business, repair charges and the charges on transport for marketing the raw material- if to be deducted from this returns that do not match up to minimum wages? For earning this type of income she works for more than eight hours on the business.

Case 2: Yasheen

Caste: Muslim

Age: 30 years

Education: studied up to seventh class.

Name of the enterprise: Specialized tailoring of Applic work on sari.

Husband's occupation: Government employee.

Owns his land

Owns three-room slab house

Husband's contribution for the enterprise is nil.

The front hall in own house used for the business.

She had no formal training and learnt tailoring from her mother.

One daughter

Private loan of Rs 25,000 @1.20 pm

1 *Enterprise*	2 *Total expenditure on raw material in a month*	3 *Earnings in a month*	4 *Total savings in a month*
Tailoring	Rs 280	Rs 560	Rs 280
Applic Chemki work	Rs 190	Rs 2000	Rs 1810

(on an average work on one piece in a month).

Total earnings 2,090 pm

Loan amount: 25,000/- @ 1.20 pm interest worked out

PM = Rs 121.70

Transport charges for getting the raw material from city

Rs 75 pm + = Rs 75.00

Total expenditure Rs 196.70

Total savings per month 1,913.30

Deduct the opportunity cost of rent Rs 1,000.00

Actual savings for the sake of daughter's marriage= Rs 913.00

Case 3

Name : Boguda Chandrakala

Caste: Guptas

Age: 40 years

Education: Studied up to fourth class.

Name of the enterprise: (multiproduct business) Grocery Kirana and general stores, cloth business and sale of bangles.

Husband's occupation is also working in the same business.

Whether he owns farm land: No.

Whether s/he owns a house: Yes s/he owns a three-room slab house

Husband's contribution for the enterprise: Business in the same kirana shop.

Business site: Her own house. The front hall is used for the business.

She had no formal training but it is their caste occupation .

Children: One daughter

SBI loan of Rs 70,000 @12% PA to repay in 50 instalments

Total interest worked out= Rs 8,400 PA=Rs 700 pm

1 *Enterprise*	2 *Total expenditure on cloth purchased in a month*	3 *Turnover in a month*	4 *Total savings in a month*
Cloth business	Rs 6,000	Rs 6,500	Rs 500
Bangles sale	Rs 200	Rs 240	Rs 40
Kirana general stores	Rs 10,000	Rs 12,000	Rs 2,000

Total earnings PM= Rs 2,540
Rent as imputed value Rs 1,000+ interest PM 1,700
Actual earnings on all three activities PM Rs 840

The above case studies tell us that the access to small increases in income may come at the cost of heavier workload and use of ancestral immobile property-house and acquired skills from informal methods. As a result, women face considerable hardship to meet loan re-payment and it has intensified tensions. From this condition of the SHG under IKP, the SHGs mobilized by the corporate MFI sector in the village worked as follows:

Case 1: Name of the respondent Ramalaxmi: For a question how did you come to know about the MFI? She responded that the MFI staff from Spandana, Basix and SKS approached her. They asked her for which enterprise the loan is required. She replied that the loan is needed for the business of making the gold ornaments by her son. After finding one person the MFI staff identifies the other four or the respondent herself identifies the remaining four members who want to work in a similar business. A very ghastly and specific to this micro finance and quite opposite to the above examples of multiproduct business on IKP the multiple corporations of microfinance institutions lent loans to the person.

The respondent raised a loan from three MFIs

Name of the MFIs:	Spandana	Basix	SKS
Amount in Rs	20,000	15,000	40,000
Date of loan availed	10-09-2009	06-8-2010	10-5-2011

(Source: Pass books issued by the microfinance institutions)

Table 1. Spandana MFI Details of Loan Repayment of Rs 20,000 by Ramalaxmi

Payment on 1	*Rs EMS 2*	*Rs PPI* 3*	*Interest 2-3= 4*	*Balance 5*
10-9-09	1500	1034	466	18966
10-10-09	1500	1110	390	17856
10-11-09	1500	1121	379	16735
10-12-09	1500	1156	344	15579
10-01-09	1500	1169	331	14410
10-02-09	1500	1194	306	13216
10-03-09	1500	1247	253	11969
10-04-09	1500	1246	254	10723
10-05-09	1500	1280	220	9443
10-06-09	1500	1299	201	8144
10-07-09	1500	1333	167	6811
10-08-09	1500	1355	145	5456
10-09-09	1500	1384	116	4072
10-10-09	1500	1416	84	2656
10-11-09	1500	1444	56	1212
10-12-09	1237	1212	25	Nil
Total	23737	20,000	3737	

*principle amount

(Total loan –Equal Monthly Instalments (EMI)+interest= column 5 balance to be paid)

The pass book given by MFI has recorded the details of total amount to be paid in each monthly instalment. Sixteen instalments are stipulated in which the total loan amount of Rs 20,000 and interest to be repaid. The total amount to be paid is worked out as Rs 23,737. This includes, the principal amount Rs 20,000 and the interest amount of Rs 3,737. The balance is arrived at by deducting Rs 1,500 the EMI from the total loan availed of and interest is worked out. The subsequent balance amounts are worked out by deducting EMI and adding the interest amount to the remaining balance (after deduction of Rs 1,500). Both Table 1 and Table 2 are worked out in this formula. **The interest amount is added each time in the total instalment and also in the balance.**

Over and above this interest rate, overhead costs are collected separately before the loan is sanctioned. It is observed that the principal amount increases as the time passes from the date of loan availed; against this the interest amount is decreasing. These types of calculations are used to create scope to work out a higher rate of interest on the increasing principal amount. Based on these calculations, the equal monthly instalments are worked out. The second loan of Rs 15,000 is raised that needs to be paid in 16 instalments.

Table 2: Basix MFI Details of Loan Repayment of Rs 15,000 by Ramalaxmi

Date to pay	*Rs EMI#*	*RS PP**	*Interest*	*Balance*
06-08-2010	1,200	655	513	14,345
06-09-2010	1,200	876	292	14,345
06-10-2010	1,200	902	266	13,469
06-11-2010	1,200	912	256	12,567
06-12-2010	1,200	938	230	11,655
06-01-2011	1,200	950	218	10,717
06-02-2011	1,200	969	199	8,767
06-03-2011	1,200	1,006	162	7,792
06-04-2011	1,200	1,009	159	6,783
06-05-2011	1,200	1,034	134	5,749
06-06-2011	1,200	1,051	117	4,698
06-07-2011	1,200	1,075	93	3,623
06-08-2011	1,200	1,094	74	2,529
06-09-2011	1,200	1,116	52	1,413
06-10-2011	1,200	1,140	28	273
06-11-2011	311	273	06	0
Total	15000		2799	

#Rs EMI equal monthly instalment *Rs PP principal amount

A third loan of Rs 40,000 is availed of from Asmitha on 10-5-2011. This amount is to be repaid with Rs 950 **equal weekly instalments** in 50 weeks. The third loan is very high and it overlaps with the second and its repayment of instalment period is per week. This heavy financial burden pushes the borrower to suicide. The clients cited the following reasons for their borrowings from micro finance.

1. Without their efforts, MFI came to their doorsteps offering the loan.
2. There was no need for them to attend any meetings held by MFI.
3. The respondents stated that they needed a convenient system of weekly repayment which the government programmes have not factored into. For the activities like vegetables, fruits, flowers and grocery (kirana) business they needed on finance on short duration. Therefore their returns are short and instalments to be paid are also short. This they think reduces the risk on their business.
4. They stated that the MFIs have no ceiling and restrictions on the amounts borrowed. They added that MF institutions simultaneously give loans to the same borrower.

Conclusions

The Self-Help Groups (SHG) programme started as subsidy-cum-loan to thrift groups in a cooperative structure by the government with the finances of the World Bank in the name of 'Velugu'. The state claimed that this programme has been initiated for eradication of poverty and empowerment of women. This has been encouraged under a "new paradigm of development" that targets women Self-Help Groups for (so-called) aid. This paradigm of development was encouraged extensively by bringing it under the policy priority of the bank's lending, by providing a new subsidy on interest called the 'Pavala Vaddy scheme.' Incentives like granting of gas cylinders was factored into the programme.

The study finds that over a decade the Self-Help Groups initiated by the government were shifted to an NGO. The NGO has expanded this programme extensively and changed its entire structure, scale of resources, level of operation and scope of functions. The financial institutions under the World Bank through this programme of SHG strengthened their monopoly power over the national and regional financial market.

The objective of this programme taken up by the state as—eradication of poverty. This objective remained unchanged in spite of transfer of the programme to NGO. The critical analysis of the empirical data shows that the world financial institutions with nexus of the Indian state initiated the programme and expanded the business in finances for the accumulation of capital. The study also consistently shows that these institutions are reducing the role of the state in the financial decision-making by acquiring monopoly over the financial market in the country. These dimensions are brought out by the study with the empirical evidences.

The state had to play a spectator role when the policies promulgated by the state were violated. While the state originally had formulated the policy of the SHG loans for creating assets that support livelihoods of women. The monopoly finance made the state include the consumption borrowings in SHG loans, subverting the asset building goal. This is evident from the data that more than 75 per cent of the sample borrowers diverted their loan amount from asset creation to consumption and the no new asset creation. That the financial institutions did not desire the poor building assets that would make them independent. For the continuation of financial business the institutions want the SHGs to be entangled in the programme.

The inclusion of consumption loan in the programme was not only to expand the business in finance but to get a hold on all earnings of the households. The data shows that a majority in the SHGs do not earn incomes. These borrowers (even in the village) were unemployed (housewives) and they necessarily depend on incomes earned by the husband or other earning members of the family for repayment of the loans. In this context it is important to note that the programme collects all the details of all household members including earning members in the membership form and make them all guarantors for repayment of the loan. This is how the entire household is netted into the programme.

The field data shows that the total amount for grounding an income earning scheme has always been less than !!!. The study shows this amount has gone down in the IKP project. The policy envisages that the enterprise is expected to earn an additional income but addition to what is not clear.

The policy norm is to mobilize the savings of the SHG members to form this ratio of one-fourth of the bank loan. But the financial institutions subverted this norm and influenced the actual mobilization of savings to a ratio of four times to that of bank loans by increasing the periodical minimum to be saved.

The case studies on government's SGSY show that their funds were shifted in the name of the community investment funds to the IKP project. These funds were meant for allotment of the subsidy component to weaker sections. The financial institutions influenced the state to shift them to develop the infrastructure, training and skills to the rojgars. These financial institutions also demanded to change this cluster rojgar programme to an individual one and they also demanded to limit the role of the state to that of facilitator. These trends explain that the financial business already expanded sufficiently to dictate terms to the state. The working of the micro enterprises under the community development funds have shown the following trends.

The micro-enterprises identified for government subsidy-cum-bank loan for weaker sections are found weak both financially and organizationally. The banks chose those enterprises to lend that have been in operation for more than 15 years. The data shows that the borrowers are also not interested in expansion of their business with these additional borrowings, on account of the market constraints. The study has shown that the banks provide these loans to those families where there are more number of earning members who can stand as guarantors. The study confirmed that the borrowers use the loan for contingent expenditures of households and not for new production or growth of employment.

The study shows these weak informal microenterprises are built on support of social institutions, guilds like SHGs that have organizations of collective economic interests and use the social capital of community life. For instance the micro-enterprises have shown that the husband purchases raw-materials for the wife's enterprise and repairs the machines in the enterprise. All the microenterprises in the study have shown that they are using the house premises for setting up the enterprise, etc. Such services of these institutions are not accounted for market value and such additional value generated help for capital accumulation. For instance a simple exercise on the pattern of interest collection by the IKP shows to Rs 16,530 per group on a loan of Rs 50,000 at the end of the fourth year this is because of the norm set by IKPas compulsory waiting period for one and half years. The other consecutive loans are on the higher side.

The SHG programme has been modified in many respects after it is shifted to IKP. For instance, the earlier SHGs were informal bodies. Now they are registered. The SHGs are linked from village to district level bodies. However the problems experienced by the members of the SHG like illiteracy (48%) continued through the decades.

On the development of the positive side of the SHG policy shows is that it has developed into a strong social force and diluted the domestic violence. However, this social power was an unintended result.

The NGOs that were registered as institutions under "public purpose" non-profit institutions turned into microfinance institutions after the reforms were implemented in the financial market by the Reserve Bank of India (MFI). These non-profit organizations obtained the Non-Banking Company status to widen their financial resource base for doing business. These institutions borrow from banks at a lower rate of interest to lend at a higher rate to SHGs.

The case studies on Pavala Vaddi, under IKP in the village shows hardly any substantial loan borrowing were going for setting up of micro enterprises. In this case there is hardly any generation of new employment. The enterprises that are set up yield very low income. The lending by microfinance is clear that the it is for business of financial institutions. A new programme has been initiated by the state called The Livelihood Mission. It advocated that the SHGs should spread into interior rural areas to eradicate poverty. The study highlights with emphasiz that SHG would only help for expansion of capital in many ways rather than for the eradication of poverty.

Suggessions: The poverty alleviation programme should be composed only with ownership of productive assets skills for the women. Skill development should be considered after asset ownership.

The financial market should be under the state and programmes like SHG should strictly be used to make assets.

NOTES

1. These are collateral groups of women with 15 members in each group to avail of credit facility from the Bank.
2. Reasons for targeting women are said to be for gender equality, for human rights, for economic, social and political empowerment. It is also stated that for transformation of power relations throughout society. For development of self-sustaining participatory women's organizations linked to a wider women's movement, for transformation of gender relations. It is said the credit is an integrated poverty-targeted community development programme which facilitates the eradication of higher levels of female poverty and for holding responsibility for household well-being. Women's empowerment is said to be more than economic empowerment and more than well-being benefits, addressing 'strategic gender interests'. Linda Mayoux *Women's Empowerment versus Sustainability? Towards a New Paradigm in Micro Finance Programmes* argues this, in a book edited by Beverly Lemire, Ruth Pearson and Gail Campbell, Berg, Oxford, New York 2001.

3. **Objectives of IKP:** The stated objective of Indira Kranthi Padham is to enable the rural poor, particularly the poorest of the poor in AP to improve their livelihoods and quality of life by facilitating formation of self-sustainable institutions of the poor. Support investments in sub-projects proposed by SHGs, VOs, and MSs.
   - Improve access to education for girls to reduce the incidence of child labour among the poor.
   - Support to disabled persons through social mobilization and access to livelihood opportunities.
   - Build capacities of established local institutions, especially the Gram Sabha/Gram Panchayat and line departments, to operate in a more inclusive manner in addressing the needs of the poor.
   - Achieve convergence of all anti-poverty programmes, policies, projects and initiatives at state, district, mandal and village levels. Payment of interest charged by banks over and above 3% per annum, subject to the maximum ceiling of 6%, provided that there is 100% repayment of the loan by Self-Help Groups is called 'Pavala Vaddi' programme. The loan accounts that are classified as overdue (during September 30th and March 31st) in the books of the bank at the time of half-yearly closing and that which are classified as Non-performing Assets at the year-end closing are not considered for the interest subsidy.
4. Chief Minister Mr. Chandrababu Naidu started the Self-Help Group (SHG) programme in Andhra Pradesh (AP) under the banner of Empowerment of Women.
5. See Annexure 1.
6. *Soumitra Kumar Bera* Financial Sector Reforms and Institutional Credit Flows for the agriculture sector in India: An analysis of its magnitude and impact (MFT BHU), Research Scholar Dept. of Economics NEHU, Shillong (undtaed).
7. National Rural Livelihood Mission (NRLM, 2011) states that the empowerment and poverty eradication of marginalized women should be achieved by providing direct access to credit through the SHG Radha Krishna Committee, GOI, 2010.

   6 **formation and registration of non-profit organisations in India** 1) Trust 2) Society 3) Section-25 Company Additional Licensing/Registration Source : http://www.ngosindia.com/resources/ngo_registration1.php/CAF India
8. Milford Bateman (2010) *Why Doesn't' Microfinance Work? 'The Destructive Rise of Local Neoliberalism*, Zed Books London, New York.

9. Haroon Habib Editorial, *The Hindu Daily*, April 5, 2011.
10. Ruth Pearson, *Continuity and Change-Towards a Conclusion* in book (ed) Beverly Lemire, Ruth Pearson and Gail Gampbell, Oxford, New York 2001.
11. As originally conceived microfinance is the provision of tiny loans to poor individuals who establish or expand a simple income-generating activity, thereby supposedly facilitating their eventual escape from poverty. Its advocates claim that microfinance has been critical to the fate of the poor in many developing countries, creating jobs and raising incomes in the poorest countries, helping to empower the poor specially women ...and a bottom-up economic and social development process, (Milford Bateman, *Why Doesn't MF Work?* 2010).
12. Milford Bateman, *Why Doesn't' Microfinance Work, 'The Destructive Rise of Local Neoliberalism*, Zed Books, London, New York, 2010.
14. *Investing in Social Capital Comparative Perspectives on Civil Society, Participation and Governance* (ed.) Sanjeev Prakash/Perselle, Sage, 2004.
15. This scheme benefited the poor. It is a programme where the beneficiaries are provided with a gas stove and a cylinder for cooking purposes. The identification of the beneficiary is done by the VO/Gram Sabha and recommended to the DRDA. The beneficiary has to pay Rs 225/- for a gas cylinder and the stove.
16. Vanamala (2003) Impact of Industrialization on Female Employment, Report submitted to ICSSR (Unpublished).
17. Vanamala, M. (2001). Ibid. "Social inclusion".
65. There are no fixed norms for loan amount. During the first three years, no loan is extended. Savings are kept with the bank. First loan say for example, accessed to Rs 50,000, after repayment of this a second loan say Rs 1,50,000 can be accessed. A third loan of Rs 2,00,000 can be obtained after repayment of the second.
18. The Livelihood Mission emphasizes the importance of SHGs as "for empowerment of women the coverage, quality and sustainability of poverty eradication programme through SHGs should be treated as utmost important for Women's Livelihood Mission (Radhakrishna, 2011). It is also mentioned that the SHG programme should spread into interior underdeveloped states and regions to free the poor from the clutches of moneylenders". (There is also evidence see the Annexure V that unfolds the fact that self-employed and cultivators households' are vulnerable and they together share 73% of the country's debt which forms

60% of the Indian households).

19. http://www.rd.ap.gov.in/DocIKP.html
20. The Draft HR Policy formulated for employees serving in SERP/IKP 1. There are multiple categories of employees recruited by the Society for Elimination of Rural Poverty (including to serve in the district units). Some of the project staff has been recruited by the Zilla Samakhyas and Mandal Samakhyas, under the facilitation support given by the project. These employees recruited either by the project or by the Samakhyas are drawing their remuneration from the project funds. SERP has formulated a draft HR policy for all such employees.
21. **Community Investment Fund (CIF):** The Community Investment Fund is one of the key components of the IKP Project. There are three types of subprojects namely (a) Income Generation, (b) Productive physical infrastructure and (c) Social development. The bulk of the CIF budget is for income generation. Out of the total IKP project budget, CIF is the most important component that determines the level of employment generation for the poor. CIF acts as a catalyst in capital formation at all levels including SHG, VO and MS and offers great leverage for raising bank funds. Under the micro plan based intervention strategy, CIF is a loan from MS to VO and from VO to SHG for implementing micro plans of SHGs, collective marketing and food security initiatives. However, it is a grant to VO in case of implementing social development and infrastructure development activities. The District Project Management Unit (DPMU) releases the CIF to the Mandal Samakhyas in instalments up to their mandal entitlement. It is implemented by Society for Elimination of Rural Poverty (SERP), Dept of Rural Development, Government of AP. SERP is an autonomous society registered under the Societies Act, and implements the project through District Rural Development Agencies (DRDAs) at the district level.

    2002, 2005, 2010: Increase in the base amount of savings per member from Rs 30 to Rs 50 and to Rs 100. The rate of interest charged by different banks are varied and they are as follows.

    1. Andhra Pradesh Grameena Vikas Bank 14 per cent. State Bank of India 12 per cent

    3. Andhra Bank 12 per cent
22. **The Eligibilty for Loan:** From the starting of the SHG membership for the first six months members save at the rate of Rs 100 per member per month. This money they keep rotating

among members up to one year. This period is called group maturity period which helps to read amicability of the members in the group. The Assistant Project Manager (APM), Patancheru Mandal interestingly stated that this period is very important for them for successful implementation and for observation of the sustainability of the group. During this period the SHG members lend their money internally. While doing this they study and understand the realities of the background of each SHG member. Once the members understand each other on rational grounds the chances of sustainability of the group increases. This period is 18 months. After this period a group becomes eligible for the first loan of Rs 50,000, to be repayable in 24 months. After the repayment the group becomes eligible for the Second Bank Linkage. This amount is up to Rs 1,50,000 to be repayable in 24 to 36 months time. After the third linkage the member or group becomes eligible for Total Financial Inclusion. The eligibility for third bank linkage is for Rs 02 lakhs to 03.75 lakhs and subsequent bank linkages are for Rs 03 lakhs and 05 to 06 lakhs. This shows that by using the social capital existing in the community life like-mutual cooperation, trustworthiness and faith are inscribed into the programme for expanding the business in SHG.

The APM said in her interview with the researcher that the bank manager exercises its discretion in release of the amounts against the stipulated amounts in the policy. However the groups have become quite familiar with the amounts stipulated and they also use their social force to question the bank manager. Thus it is clear that IKP keeps working on expansion of its business educating the SHG that they are a ***social force and can question the banks***. Thus IKP uses the social capital of community life to earn good-will and credibility of the groups that is useful in further expansion of the business. The expansion under the bank-linkage programme is as follows.

23. Bhaskara Rao Report on National Network Enabling Self-Help Movement (NN-ABLE)2009 APMAS.
24. A National Network Enabling (NN-ABLE) the SHG movement was formed in 2007 with the financial support of the Ford Foundation. The Ford Foundation has been funding to promote models for up scaling and replication. The NN-ABLE has worked out the minimum seed capital requirement for an enterprise to be viable. It is assessed that an investment of Rs 15,000 per SHG for 8 to 10 years will promote effective livelihood opportunities

and would yield Rs 2000/additional income per Swarojgar per month.

25. Ibid., 49.
26. Reddy, Y.V. (2009), "India's Financial Sector in Current Times" *Economic and Political Weekly*, November 7.
27. *The Hindu*, Friday January 21, 2011.
28. *Indian Express,* April 26, 2011, p. 1.
29. EPW Research Foundation, *EPW*, May 28, 2011, Vol XLVI, No. 22.

6

Case Study of the Manufacturing Industry-PENNAR

Introduction: The last chapter on the Self-Help Groups' movement known as 'a new paradigm of development', targeting female labour, for providing livelihood occupations has shown that it has turned into financial business. The state started this development programme with World Bank funds and entrusted it to an NGO for operation. It has enlarged the programme by deepening and widening the scale of financial operations. It has developed its own organizational and managerial and employment hierarchic structures. Such a change provided huge scope for doing financial business with the support of the state. The NGOs that were started with philanthropic funds in the country have joined the financial business through SHGs and widened financial sources by shifting into the Non-Bank-Financial-Company status. The corporate microfinance companies also joined this programme (SHGs) for their financial business. These developments explain that the programme of SHG was started for expansion of financial business and not for creating assets and development of skills for livelihood sustenance. These institutions pushed the SHG women into debt cycles. The new paradigm of development has not provided livelihood support to female labour. The development strategy that displaced and deskilled women in argarian sector claims to have created more employment opportunities to female labour in the new industrial policy.

The present study probed into the employment of female labour in new industries. This study tracks the employment of displaced female labour from land (older generation) from the village under study young educated migrant female labour. It is alarming to find only older generation from the village. The present study on a manufacturing industry is an attempt to enquire into the opportunities of employment and quality of work life of young migrant female labour in new industrial employment. A brief review of literature of the earlier studies on the new industrial employment provides a basic frame for analysis.[1]

Mark Holmstorm (1984)[2] and Gerry Rodger (2007)[3] argue that the new industries expand the hired informal workers to a proportion equal to their decided capital accumulation.[4] For accumulation of capital these industries adopted cost cutting strategies on labour.

The tasks developed by the multi technology in new industries are so simplified that they can be picked up on-the-job by the less educated or by even illiterates. This type of technology is invented as has been stated by scholars that this type of developments in technology that justify the lower payments in the insecure employment particularly to women as most of them are illiterates.

The scholars observed that the employment in new industries is informal hired employment that increased or stretched the working hours[5] of female labour from the stipulated number of working hours. They also emphasized that these industries cut the labour costs, depress wages, curb labour power and voice of the workers in new labour relations (Vanamala, 2002).

They argued that such work does not provide economic security and social dignity required for "Decent"[6] work (Vanamala 2002).

Pyke and Sengenburger observed that these industries use the flexible labour. This they stated is to achieve two goals of the industry. One, to cut the labour costs which the authors called the Low-road-model or the "destructive model". They observed that this low-road-model offers poor wages in low social conditions. They stated that the second model is the "High-road-model" or the "constructive model", is based on considerations of efficiency and innovations of workers. Holmstrom (1998) analysed these two models and observed that the developing countries have surplus labour and is available on cheap wage offers. He added emphasis that the cheapest labour is female unskilled labour. Therefore it is possible for industries to **prioritize accumulation of capital** by employing female labour for their own expansion with the support of the state. Therefore he confirmed that the adoption of the high-road-model in these countries is not possible. He cautioned those countries adopting the low-road-model by stating that it is a **social cost on labour** that effects labour adversely for a long time to come. With this backdrop of the studies the following interview of the Human Resource manager of the industry under the case study has to be understood.

Human Resources: The Changing Trends in Pennar

The industry Nagarjuna Steels Ltd, a sick industrial unit, was purchased by Pennar to produce steel, automobiles, refrigerators, air conditioners and other engineering products. The Nagarjuna Steels had employed permanent workers and had strong labour unions. It was working as an import substation for steel catering to the needs of the local market like Godrej India Ltd. Its share of exports was confined to developing countries like Nepal and Bhutan. After the merger of Nagarjuna Steels with Pennar, the industry that had specialized in cold rolling facility has restructured into the privatized, liberalized and globalized market by changing its organizational, operational, technical and managerial systems. The industry, had to opt for restructuring (as stated by the HR manager) to rescue itself from the crisis that hit the steel industry worldwide during 1999 to 2002.

The manager HR stated that to make the industry cost effective as part of restructuring into the new liberalized economy it had to suspend social security provisions like 'the canteen subsidy, pay revisions and flight conveyance, PF, and ESI' to its permanent staff. These social security provisions were replaced with new incentives that increased the productivity of the workers. The new measures focused were gauging the efficiency of workers to cope with the **new technical *scale of operations*,** diversification of industry into multi-products manufacturing along with intensification of R&D and maintenance of quality of product. As a part of this the production was diversified into tubes for automobiles. A new metal 'Mile' steel was introduced for railways.

The old labour intensive methods of Taylorism/Fordism were replaced with new capital intensive and multi-tasking technology. The mass production technology has been replaced with the Just-in-time and Just-in-case[7] that is to produce in small quantities on customer demand has been introduced. The permanent workers of Nagarjuna Steels were terminated and employed workers on flexible, casual and contractual and feminized basis. The manager stated that, they had to terminate the services of even the skilled and permanent workers in the old structure enforcing the Voluntary retirement scheme. He maintained that 80 per cent of them were reinstated after three years on changed conditions of "getting down some steps in salary and social security provisions". A respondent stated that about 300 workers left the industry to work in Saudi Arabia, West Indies and Goa. He maintained that they are settled in better conditions compared to their own.

At present the restructured Pennar is a major industry with eight production departments namely, Engineering Component Division (ECD), Cold Rolling (CRFC), Human Resources, Electrical Engineering, Mechanical, Fabrication, Production Planning Control and Quality Control, that work in three shifts. Each department is headed by a manager and a supervisor that possessed a certificate of engineering (from the Institution of Engineers). The categories of supervisor are two types; one, operating supervisors who work on machines and two, the non-operating supervisors. Below the supervisors formal, permanent and high skilled operators are placed. The promotion cadres of operators were ranked in A, B, and C grades based on the length of their service. This promotion was only in monetary benefits without any elevation in position. The industry specialized in metallurgy with Rs 1,000 crore turnover and employed 1,400 employees along with 600 casual workers.

The manager observed the turnover of labour in the industry is at two extreme labour ends; one, at a level of highly skilled engineers and the other level is the level of unskilled physical labour. To arrest these turnovers, the industry introduced new incentives like- the best attendance awards, awards to workers who have completed 10, 15, 20 and 25 years of service. The workers were provided one casual leave for a service of every 20 days. New earned leaves were introduced for each of the festivals and along with 10 sick leaves. To attract unskilled workers, a worker is offered one earned leave for every 20 days of physical work. The manager stated that although the retirement age is 58 years, more than 80 per cent of them were retained on the job. The manager ostensibly noted that the company is retaining them even after their retirement as a favour. However the fact is that the industry was trying to retain the workers who are highly skilled having long service. This combination produces quality products for the international market to make huge profits. The industry is providing the social security measures to retain the skilled workers that are industry specific.

The Nagarjuna Steels had a very strong Trade Union under the state regulation system. This union is replaced with the collective bargain system after its merger with Pennar. This body of collective bargain meets once in three years to bargain on the service conditions and social security benefits like House Rent Allowance (HRA), Educational benefits, medical insurance[8], gratuity, PF, leaves and accident insurance. As these[9] skilled workers are profession-specific, no efforts were made by the industry to train the new staff. In such a situation the industry had to depend on existing skilled workers and as the skill is industry-specific the workers had to depend on industry (mutually dependent). It is made clear in the words of the respondent that *"the nature of work I am doing, does not allow me to change the job. He maintained that his work involves high level skill in gauging of metal, this has been acquired on-the-job. In the same vein the producer cannot get-rid- of us as this skill is not available in the market and therefore he stated industry has accepted for execution of some labour laws"*. This explains that inspite of probability of high risk in availability of skilled workers; the industry is not training the new labour, as industry considers training only expenditure on labour.

The industry Pennar had employed a range of workers like permanent, contract, casual employees that have a long association with the working of the industry under the industrial policies of both regulated and deregulated markets in its eight departments. After the 1990s restructuring of industry into the globalized market, it opened a department called Engineering Component Department (ECD) that employed more number of female labourers in the first two production shifts. This division is selected as a case study to inquire into the working conditions of labour in general and working conditions of female labour in particular. This study on ECD is a continuation of a case study done by the scholar on a similar industry—BPL, in 1995-96. As the BPL is closed down, the study on ECD is substituted to track as both the industries worked under similar conditions of labour laws and technology into the changes in the labour relations and working conditions in the last three decades.

The Engineering Component Division (ECD) shows that the female workers outnumbered the male workers. The female workers were placed at the tail end in the hierarchy of industrial workers. The female labour employed include from illiterates to the education level who have completed 10th class. The educated female labour was equal in qualification to that of permanent workers at their respective entry points.

The structure of the ECD is organized in a **pyramid shape** with personnel in four ranks. On the top is the Manager of the division under whom two **technically qualified male permanent status engineers** in the capacity of supervisors work. Under them the experienced operators called **staff** (full-fledged machine operators and quality controllers called staff) who have put in a total service of more than five years are placed. Out of this experience of five years they have worked two years as contract employees. During this period they learnt on-the-job skills to work on all machines[10]. Under the staff contract labour are placed. Below them the casual labour or helpers work (The respondents stated that there is no difference in work status of contract and casual workers). From the following figure it is clear that in the last rank the casual and contract workers are largest in number. The comparison of ECD structure with BPL shows that the top technical persons can be reduced in number by replacement of workers with capital intensive automatic machines. The organizational structure of the workers in both ECD and BPL are as follows.

Pyramid shape of workers' organization in ECD.

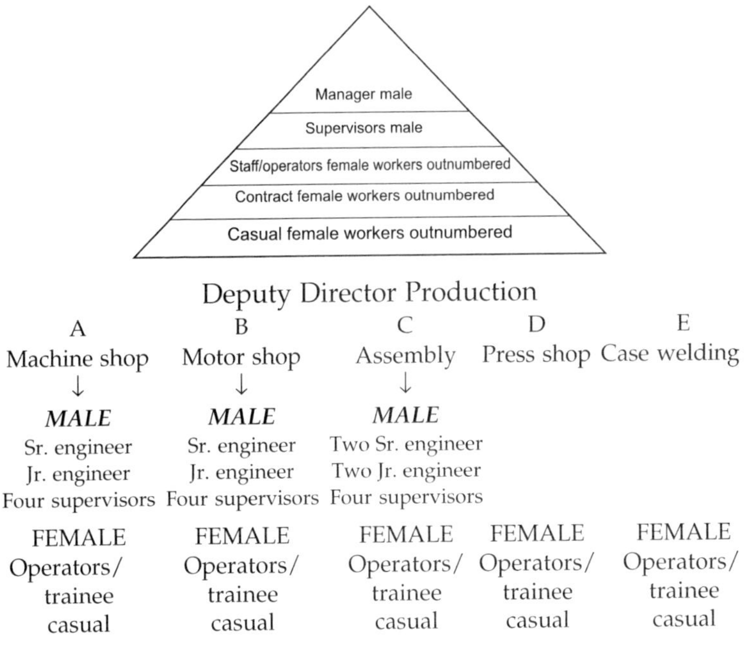

The role of each rank and file in ECD is as follows.

Role of Manager in ECD: The Manager (male) is the first rank person over these female informal workers in ECD. He assesses the "attitude", "planning" and "performance" of the workers to place them in "good" "better" and "best" ranks and sends his assessment report to Human Resource (HR) Department. Based on this report the manager HR decides whether the increments to be given to the worker. The increments begin from Rs 500 enhancement in wages per annum per worker. These measures for assessment of performance do not help scientifically to arrive at objective standards.

The manager (ECD) maintains that the difference in work allocation is negligible and in terms of turn-over of output, no difference is observed between male and female workers. He said that the wages paid are equal to the both workers. However, he emphasized that "in terms of 'concentration on the work', the female labour is more "**promising**". This word mentioned by the manager needs further probing.

He stated that there is no fixed amount for increment, no fixed time period for offering it to the workers. He observed that the actual criteria of promotion are based on the growth of the production. However, he stated that a worker is put in the casual status for a minimum of two to three years. After completion of this period, a casual worker becomes an operator. When the worker becomes an operator or staff, S/he, will be eligible for pay-slip, Provident Fund (PF)[11] Employees State Insurance (ESI), increments, Bonus, leaves, transport benefits facility and gifts on annual family day, celebrated by the industry.

This explains that a small number of workers of staff category are maintained. While the contract and casual workers will be increased along with increase in the demand of the product they are producing. This explains that most of the production for industry is with very low payments and without any payments of social security benefits to contract and casual workers.

The respondents felt that despite long service on operations of machines, the ECD structure did not have provision for their promotions. They complained that it is unjust on the part of industry to link their promotion with the market demand for their products. They pointed out that when industry recruited them to do work given by industry against this, how is it justified linking their promotions with market? They also stated that they work under contract worker relations as long as the industry wishes them to keep on the rank without any upgradation even in monetary benefit.

Female workers shared their observation and stated that the discrimination in operating promotions is obvious when compared with the male workers within the ECD division. The higher pay and increment is fixed for male workers. The manual work (like loading and unloading) is fixed at a higher level. However from the following narration it is evident that the senior staff cadre working in ECD did think that women are discriminated against as there was a difference in wages. This woman working in the senior staff cadre in ECD observes:

> that sixty female along with fifty male workers have been working in ECD with 30:80 regular and casual workers. She became an operator since the last three years. There is no change in her status of work except monetary benefit. Every year her salary is increased by Rs 380. She draws Rs 4,500 per month at present. Out of this Rs 250 deducted for canteen and Rs 200 towards PF.

She further stated that the most vulnerable poor are working in their division which is clear from the fact that 90 per cent of workers depend on subsidized canteen food. She stated that male workers are seniors in ECD. They draw higher salary over female workers. Generally males do not prefer working in ECD, it is known as the girls division.

She is also aware of working conditions in other industries which are workse. She observed that female workers in their industry are respected also compared to others. She observed that although work is heavy in this division, workers do like the industry as the work is based on rules and payments are decent and respectable compared to other industries. Every OT is paid double the amount. Although the industry does not fix any targets to production, the supervisor sets the automatic machines that are different in the capacity of manufacture. Some machines manufacture one piece per minute; other machines can produce two pieces per minute. Work is heavy as ECD undertakes subcontract work. She also knows that such intensive work does not allow workers to pursue higher education and training. She expressed her own experience stating that although she paid the fee to take the Open University exam she could not make it on account of work pressure in the industry. This explains that the industry is concerned with its own production but not labour skill formations. This is further confirmed by her helplessness when she stated that,

"Every Saturday industry holds a meeting to discuss the profit and loss of the division and to serve the work orders. Every step of industry revolves around growth in the production. For instance the industry celebrates annual family day, and gifts are offered to inspire staff workers for committed work."

Coming back to the organizational structure, as has already been stated that the supervisors are placed below the manager to attend the following functions.

Functions of Supervisor: The daily work allotment is done by the section supervisors. The promotion of the **staff cadre** is based on the supervisor's confidential reports and attendance. The confidential report is about the efficiency of the workers. Although the targets for production are not served on paper to the workers, the ECD machines have an inbuilt capacity of 600 pieces of turnover per day. The measurement of work is based on these production units and thus the efficiency of the workers.

Operators: As has already been stated the operators are hierarchically of two types. The senior operators are 'staff'. They are directly under industry. Next to them are operators under the 'labour contractor'. The ECD workers work on all 365 days in a year with automatic machines that have inbuilt-capacity.

The promotion of operators under the labour contractor

depends on the conduct report given by the labour contractor. To get one promotion from the cadre of helper (packer) to operator cadre, the worker has to put in a minimum of two to three years of service under the contractor. During this period they learn operations of multi-machines on-the-job (contributing to productions). The salary paid to them is Rs 150 per head per day by the contractor. This amount is equal to female agricultural wages in the region in off season (during the season female agricultural wages are Rs 250). This is striking that the wages paid by the BPL industry were equal to the then agricultural wages in 1995-96 (see for details Vanamala, 2003)[12]

Out of the wages of Rs 150 per day an amount of Rs 12 are deducted for breakfast and lunch served in the industry. Out of the remaining Rs 138, the worker has to bear transport charges. Below the contract labour, the casual labour is placed in the production pyramid. These casual helpers are also supplied by the labour contractor. These workers are not eligible for availing any infrastructure and social security benefits of the industry like, transport, ESI card and Provident Fund benefits. The institution of labour contractor is a new structure came up after the year 2000 in new industries. The analysis on the impact of this organization is presented as follows. (during the study of BPL it did not exist).

The Institution of Labour Contractor: This is an institutional arrangement for the supply of required number of casual labour for the day's production just in time. The quantity of labour changes depending on the day-to-day demand for production for that particular product. The labour contractor supplies casual/contract workers to supplement the existing staff on pay rolls to balance the labour needed for that day. He is a license holder to supply labour on contract and casual basis to the industry. He deposits fee with the labour officer based on the number of workers for which he seeks permission to supply. The industry has to pay him a commission of Rs 6 per worker on the number of labour supplied per day. The casual and contract workers are placed under the unskilled category. They are promoted to junior staff after working for a minimum of two to three years. The salaries to these workers are paid by the labour contractor[13] based on his assessment of efficiency of the worker.

The "attitude" of worker "attendance" and "behaviour" of the worker are informal discursive measures to certify the efficiency of the labour. At the end of the month the labour contractor certifies the man days worked by contract/casual workers for payment of salary for the month. The late reporting on duty by a worker is treated as absent. All these practices show the power and exploitative working conditions of the contractor over the casual and contract workers. The exploitation of contract and casual workers are practised as follows.

The respondents stated that for the period of contract service the workers are not given any identity cards, employment order or salary slips or particularly receipts for the amounts deducted towards PF for which workers are legitimately entitled. The workers are informed that the deductions towards PF indicate their continuation in work unlike the casual workers, for whom the PF contribution is not offered and continuation of their employment is uncertain. However, the workers observed that the PF deducted from salaries of contract labour is never paid to anyone including those who have stopped working in the industry. To claim it, they neither have any evidence from the contractor or support from the industry. The workers think that the payment of commission for supply of labour by the contractor to the industry is adjusted from these deductions. For such actions of the labour contractor the industry (a principal employer) is indifferent. This type of "informal cost cuttings on labour" by the labour contractor cannot be traced as industry is indifferent. The new industries have managed to get changed the labour laws, particularly of the contract laws to favor their own expansion through cost cutting on labour with support of the state.[14] The following sample study on the Pennar industry reveals the real processes of industry in cost cuttings through the expansion in informalized, feminized, segmented and hierarchical production structure for female labour.

The cost cutting is observed in the system of recruitment of workers in the industry. The industry uses the social structures such as caste, community and personal relations are used for selection of workers. These are institutions that enhance the capital accumulation through cost cutting on those factors.

Method of Recruitment in Industry: The good-will of worker and social structures are used for recruitment of the fresh lot by the industry. This method of recruitment provides loyalty from workers and safety to the industry. The sample data shows the following patterns.

ECD recruitment is based on the contacts and contractor.

	Labour contractor	*Relatives*	*Senior workers*	*Self*	*Total*
1	2	3	4	5	6
ST	2	0	0	0	2
SC	3	3	1	0	7
BC	15	1	7	4	27
OC	6	5	7	3	21
Total	26	9	15	7	57

Source: Field data from respondents

The data on the recruitment mechanism of the workers shows that as many as about 47 per cent are recruited through the formal channel of labour contractor while more than 53 per cent is recruited through social structures. Out of this more than 41 per cent of the workers were recruited by kith and kin who are already working in the industry. Twelve per cent of them approached the industry on their own for recruitment. This explains that the social capital of the community life is used by industry.

The recruitment of workers that approach the industry on their own suggests that migration, poverty and vulnerability of the workers were one of the push factors for recruitment. The living conditions of the workers recruited is evident from the socio-economic conditions of the family and other family members. The educational particulars of the other family members also another indicator of the workers recruited. The educational levels of family members shows that they are either illiterates or have completed primary level education.

The data on the occupational details of family members of the workers recruited shows that mother/elderly women are housewives, fathers engaged in precarious and insecure employment like masons, security guards, agriculture, self-employed, etc. More than 63 per cent of them earn an income of less than Rs 100 per day. This explains that the poverty and vulnerability has been compelling the young educated girls to work in the company under unfavorable working conditions. The poverty is more intense among the migrant households. More than 70 per cent of workers migrated from various far and near rural villages. The reason for migration reveals that more than 72 per cent migrated to seek employment. The migration increased the supply of young educated labour enormously. With this excess supply of labour the industry kept on expanding the casual and contractual workers that work in lower cadres as unskilled for very low payments.

More than 75 per cent of the workers that migrated do not own a house in the place of destination. Forty-two per cent of the workers pay a rent of Rs 1,500 or less while seven per cent of them are paying between Rs 1,500-2,500. Because of migration this heavy expenditure on housing is an additional burden on the workers. The house rent allowances are paid by the industry to only 37 per cent of the staff cadre. The casual and contractual cadres are not eligible for this allowance whose number has been expanded regularly. The unmarried male workers share the living space to save on rent. The problem of residence is so critical that it should connect to the pick-up points of workers by industrial transport. The shelter in the township is unaffordable. For those who stay in the outskirts transport is a problem. However as has been mentioned the lower two cadres who are more in number are not eligible for transport expenses. These are the other devices of cost cutting on labour.

The data reveals that the mechanism of cost cutting on labour have been increasing in the last 20 years. This is presented with the help of a case study done by the scholar in 1995-96. The BPL manufacturing, export-oriented formal industry that was producing compressors and motor parts by recruiting young educated unmarried female labour in the informal division (of the formal industry BPL) have been selected to look at the changes in working conditions of female labour in Pennar (as a continuation of BPL in last 30 years). As the BPL industry is closed down, the industry Pennar also recruits female labour on similar patterns in the informal division which helps for disclosing comparative changes in the manufacturing industry.

Conditions for Recruitment: The BPL used to recruit unmarried girls in the age group of 16-18, who completed school final education. They were recruited ostensibly on training by paying stifund. The industry recruited male and more number of female labour in informal divisions of the industry only on two cadres namely, contractual and casual. They were recruited through daily newspaper advertisements and drawn the labour from local and neighbouring villages. By 2009-10 the Pennar industry recruited female labour in the age group of more than 25 years to 45 year, married female workers. More than 68 per cent of them are married and live with spouses. The unmarried female workers live with parents. To cut the costs educational levels were further downgraded and even illiterates were also recruited limiting the qualification to the school final as the upper limit. Formal and informal institutions were created for recruitment. About 50 per cent of workers were recruited through contract labour institutions and the other half was done through relatives and friends that are already working in the industry.

Increase in Informal Cadres and Intensity of Technology Over Period: Pennar increased the informal cadres to three levels—like staff, contractual and casual. The system of multi-tasking and diversification has been widened and intensified with the number of machines to be operated and products manufactured. The earlier BPL industry manufactured only two types of products, while the Pennar increased this to twelve types of products on machines. The products include fridge cells, AC machine parts, electrical engineering components, CH, LH and UH hole making (centre, lower and upper hole), foreman, machine operator, bore well pumps, construction of material parts and quality control, scooter parts. The sample data on the production particulars shows that the workers are also given sub-contract work in the hydraulics division. The workers stated that they work for all 365 days of the year, the company never suffers the short of work for this division. The value of production has been growing consistently as has been stated by the manager of ECD. This explains that there has been an increase in intensity of multi-tasking with higher capital intensive technology. The production has been expanding with employment based on market demand for products. Therefore production is based on highly flexible casual employment. These are achieved not only through legal sanctions from the state but also under increased coercions and compulsions. These are reflected in the following presentation.

Wages

The segregation into gendered tasks is created particularly in the lower levels that require lesser level of education. Such a technology helped the industry in cost cutting on female wages. As has been already stated the female workers are recruited from the education ranging from illiteracy to 10th class completed. The male workers were selected from those that have completed 10th class and above. The female respondents stated that the industry never created any scope to female labour to pursue their higher studies. Thus in the gendered, segregated and feminized tasks the female labour are employed and paid lower wages. These cost cuttings are going into capital accumulation.

Within the female labour another level of segregation is introduced. The lower cadre female labour is placed in the same level for two to three years with a daily payment of Rs 150. The salaried and better placed category gets Rs 167 per day (Rs 5,000-5,600 per month). This works out to 11 per cent higher wages to salaried worker over casual workers (in 2009-10). This difference between these categories of workers was 22 per cent in 1995-96. This difference in salaried and casual has been maintained at the cost of increase in the number and rung of casual workers.

Table 3: Wage Structure in Pennar

Wages in Rs per month		*Service in Years*		*Qualifications*		*Yearly Increments*	
Male	*Females*	*Male*	*Female*	*Male*	*Female*	*Male*	*Female*
6150-to 6750	5000-to 5600	2-5	2-5	10th	Illiterate to 10th	600-1000	500-650

Table (3) shows that the Pennar paid wages of Rs 150 per day to contract and casual labour. The take home salary worked out to Rs 133 per day after deduction for canteen food. This is much lower than the wages paid for agricultural workers. The casual workers are not eligible for tea while the **staff** category workers were eligible for free of cost tea. These hierarchies, segments created are for making '**super**' and **'quick'** profits by industry. In view of such payments the Supreme Court stated that- in a particular employment that does not cover the **minimum wages**, that employment should be considered illegal as it amounts to bonded labour[15] (Venugopal).[16] Against these wages paid by the Pennar industry, the wage structure of the previous industry—the BPL was as follows table (4) in 1997-98.

Table 4. Wage Structure in BPL Per Month in Rs

Cate. of worker	*1st year in Rs*	*2nd year in Rs*	*3rd year in Rs*	*per day in Rs*
Trainees	520	650	1,380	45
Casual	1,145	1,145	1,145	37

The BPL paid Rs 45 and Rs 37 per day to trainees and casual workers respectively (Table 4). The tea and subsidized food was provided to all types of workers. However the real present wages of the salaried or staff (compressed to a fraction in number) cadre increased[17] in Pennar over what BPL has paid to its salaried. However the wage bill as a whole of the female workers decreased along the progress in production, because of the expansion in number and rank in the lower daily paid workers. These are the new processes used in intensifying the capital accumulation.

The observation on increment shows that the increment in ECD starts with Rs 600 and Rs 500 for male and female workers (Rs100 difference) after the completion of service of the first year in the staff category. By the time of the third increment to the staff category the gap in the male and female wages gets widened from Rs 100 (difference in the first year) to Rs 450 due to the in-built wage structure that is adopted with variation in increments which creates a progressive gap between male and female wages. This technique helps in drawing the cheapest female labour into production with a consequent rise in capital accumulation.

The functioning of new industrialization in respect of female labour is evident from the Pennar Industry which is a formal industry set up for development of the backward region and worked for import substitution in cold rolling steel previously. It had employed permanent, skilled; industry-specific labour. To go for restructuring into liberalized and globalized economy it has retrenched them and went on expanding the scale of production and techniques of cost cutting for capital accumulation by reinstating them in the lower level employment securities. For instance, a few tasks are allotted to segregated female labour by employing a small fraction of them on long-term contract (staff). By constantly expanding the number of daily paid female labour (over the previous structure of production in BPL) at the base level along with the scale of production (see Annexure 1) has increased the exploitation of labour by cutting costs in their wages. This pattern is inherent in the very nature of capital under the new model of development. By developing a technology with the repetitive tasks and making accessible to labour with lower level education employing the cheapest labour in this country, the exploitation level has been heightened.

Conclusions: Globalized economy of course, has generated new opportunities of work for female labour; they are generated in working conditions of cost cutting on wages. The unregulated capital market knows no bounds in its own expansion (capital accumulation) by inventing methods and mechanisms of progressive cost cutting which is inversely related to hierarchy of employment. For instance, the study shows some mechanisms of cost cutting as an increase in segregated categories of workers over earlier data. The segmented workers are placed in pyramid shape, with a small fraction of the better placed workers followed by the contract and casual workers. These two lower categories are enlarged in number over better placed workers. They are placed in the segmentation of unskilled category and they work under the labour contractor. They are not considered as industrial workers and do not have any identity of industry and dignity of work that better placed workers enjoy. Though all these workers do the same work ostensibly the industry placed them under trainees for two to three years. They are paid Rs 133 per day per worker as take home wages. Such a low payment is illegal. The industry earns a minimum of Rs 1,32,120 profits with such low payments to these workers[18] for the workers' training period. These illegal earnings are arrived at based on the wages fixed for the better placed workers. These profits are earned from unfair employment which is largest in number.

The workers' promotion is not based on seniority or skills but, based on demand for products produced. Therefore, promotion has no professional norms. However, the industry states attitude, attendance and behaviour as their norms. These norms and mechanisms work as cost cutting on labour.

The industries adopt the cost cutting production methods like multi-tasking, just-in-time and just-in-case, overtime, multiple production shifts. By adopting these methods the industry earns quick profits.

The industry cuts the costs on labour by recruiting them with the help of social structures (of accumulation) like caste, relations, region, etc. The senior workers in industry use such social structures and recruit the workers for the industry.

Instead of imparting skills to the workers that are long lasting for their livelihood, the industry introduced new incentives. The incentives were introduced with dual purposes of making workers work regularly and with commitment and quick profits to industry. Some of these incentives are—the best attendance awards, awards to workers who have completed 10, 15, 20 and 25 years of service. The workers were provided one casual leave for a service of every 20 days. New earned leaves were introduced for each festival and along with 10 sick leaves. To attract unskilled workers were offered one earned leave for every 20 days of physical work. These are different segmentations of work for quick profit making.

The entire industrialization process does not ensure any absorption of labour with better conditions than the conditions of agricultural labourers. The displaced female labour coupled with the migrant labour and limited occupations variable for them and technology that is made easy accessible even for illiterates have together facilitated the industry to employ female labour on discriminatory terms at lower wages at their will and to accumulate the higher and higher level of capital. The development of employment market for female labour is such that it has not opened any new avenues and whatever avenues opened they are no better than the earlier agricultural labour.

NOTES

1. The present case study (2010) is a continuation of previous case study done in the 1990s, which was closed down on account of its unviability. The present industry is selected to continue the track of inquiry within the nexus of the state on the quality of work life of female workers. The present industry selected for the study is similar in operational, organizational and technological environment of the working female labour like in that of the previous industry 13 p. 2. This justified the methodology.
2. Mark Holmstrom (1984), *Industry and Inequality: The Social Anthropology of Indian Labour*, Cambridge University Press, Cambridge.

3. Gerry Rodger (2007), Decent Work, Social Inclusion and Development in *Indian Journal of Human Development*, Vol. 1 No. 12007. The concept of decent work originated in 1999 and explains "The employment, social protection, rights at work and social dialogue". He proposes that the 'production system should achieve both social and family goals'; also see Gerry Rodger (2007), 'Labour Market Flexibility and Decent Work' in Jose Antonio Ocampo and Jomo KS (ed) *Towards Full and Decent Employment*, Orient Longman, Published in Association with the United Nations.
4. Forty-eight per cent of the world's workers were not earning above a per capita income of $2 per day. The new types of jobs made 52.9 million wage workers dependent on the unorganized non-farm sector for their livelihood. A far more more alarming reality he brings out is that in the organized sector they constitute 76.7 million. This process is continued by setting Special Economic Zones (SEZ), displacement of peasant families by expropriating peasant proprietors' land and turning them into wage labour. This is the latest trend from 2005. These factors affect labour in general and female labour in particular.
5. Guy Standing (1986) observes five labour insecurities in flexible employment. 1. Labour market (surplus labour), employment (greater higher and fire), job insecurity (alterations of job contents), work insecurity (with health hazards) and income insecurities.
6. The World Summit on Social Development (1995) explains the meaning and importance of the "Decent" work and states that the employment was the heart of social policy.
7. Tom Hewitt, Hazel Johnson and David Wield (1992).
8. The new industries have adopted the Japanese Kanban or "Just in time" system (also Vanamala, 2003). To adopt these systems, "Flexible Specialization" decentralized production in relatively small units with subcontracting particularly in developing countries becomes the pattern of the production system.
9. These changes in the developing countries led to the 'low cost' and 'marginalized' labour markets. William Lezonic (1991), *Business Organisation and the Myth of the Market Economy*, Cambridge University Press: Cambridge.
10. The workers requested that the medical insurance should be extended to the entire family members. The second haunting problem for them is children's education. They stated at least loans should be arranged for education from KG to higher

education without charging interest.

11. The observation shows that the operations on the machines account for not less than fifty items. To name some cup-shells parts of compressors.
12. (For eligibility under ESI every worker should get one identity card for 4.75% of the industry contribution, 1.75% contribution from workers' wages for insurance Sreedhar Labor Laws (1998), Asia Law House
13. Vanamala (2003), *EPW*.
14. In 12 months, if more than 120 days of work is done it does not come under casual or contract work. Even work which is seasonal and is available for 60 days, it does not come under contract or casual work. When the work is available on a regular basis, to be done by regular workers, or when for some time work is available regularly (clarification is left to the State's decision) that work should not be done by contract workers. Contract Labour Act 1970 Sreedhar Madabhooshi (1998).
15. Industrial Employment Standing Order Act 1946. Categorization of workers: 1. Permanent 2. Probation, 3. Badilee, 4. Temporary, 5. Casual, 6. Apprenticeship. These categories have become irrelevant in new industries.
16. K.R. Venugopal (2013) live discussion with HMTV channel.
17. Ibid.
18. The index numbers of average industrial wages deflated with the consumer price index during 2009-10 has shown that the wages have increased.
19. 36 months x 5,000 =1,80,000. 30x133= 3,990x12= 47,880; 180,000-47,880= 1,32,120

7

Conclusions

The process of policy shifts and the way the Indian economy went through the shifts during the last six decades has been fairly debated. Of all the changes the critical turning point was in the early 1980s when India's approach to development started changing rapidly and that change picked up momentum from the early 1990s. The pace of change has been so rapid that some of the changes were drastic and undemocratic. The impact of urbanization and industrialization on the village economy, rural life and occupational patterns, quality of life stemmed from the work life require close and critical examination. This study on a select village at three points of time during the last three decades provides an insight into the micro-level developmental processes. The special focus has been on women as they are hit hard by this model more than men. The processes of development segmented, marginalized, feminized and exploited women across castes and classes. This provides a vantage point to see the intensity and magnitude of process of development at one level and marginalization and exploitation at another level.

The study reveals a powerful trend of commercialization of crop shifting to commoditization of farm land in the agrarian economy. This is evident from the fact that there was 1991 acres of land under the village in 1984-85. Out of it only 18 acres (which works out to less than one percent) were uncultivated and the remaining of 99 per cent of land was under cultivation. Out of it, 1671.35 acres had the benefit of water resources (wetland) and the paddy was cultivated in 1200 acres in the Kharif and 500 acres in the Rabi season in the village. The paddy crop is female labour intensive. The study shows that it engaged male and female cultivators in the ratio of 2:97 and the agricultural labour in the ratio of 0.60:1 resulting in the expansion of female farm employment. The study shows that because a majority of wetland holdings family incomes were fairly high, there was high spread of reluctance for sale of these lands. However, the land acquisition started by the Indian Infrastructure Corporation of India under the **development of the backward region** for **Garibi Hatao** (political agenda of Indira Gandhi). The total land sold initially in a period of about 20 years (1973-74 to 1990-91), was 160 acres or 12 per cent of the total land of the village.

The two state interventions to start with commercialization of paddy and industrialization through public sector undertakings that co-opted several members from the landed households. About half the village cultivators were earning fairly good incomes. This rise in incomes of the cultivator household operated as pull-out-of-hired-female-labour across class and caste at various levels of economic status. The female labour that withdrew from hired labour got confined to private space, homes as housewife (to domestic labour) triggering the process of "Housewifization". This process is reflected in the withdrawal of female labour from hired wage labour as income levels started rising.

The study shows that privatization and deregulating the market economy resulted in a high level shift of farm land to non-farm particularly in the holding category of small and marginal farmers. This happened because of the unprecedented rise in input prices (chemical fertilizers, pesticides, water, electricity), land prices and costs of agricultural services (like services of tractor) against depressed prices of agricultural output, distribution of fake agricultural seeds and non-cooperation of rice mills in paddy purchases, state imports of paddy from other states for Public Distribution, all cumulatively made paddy cultivation unviable. This got aggravated further with withdrawal of state support to infrastructural development particularly water resources which have been appropriated by the industrial estate. The cultivation was further reduced to unviable holdings by enactment of state policy that sanctioned direct loans to tenants resulting in withdrawal of sharecropping by the landed. The fully mechanized cultivation in these conditions incurred a loss of Rs 3,100 on each acre of paddy cultivation. Such conditions forced the small and marginal farmers to sell their holdings.

These unviable holdings resulted in a drastic shift into either keeping the land fallow or into sale of land that led to forced shift of female labour into non-farm occupations. These shifts of land and labour adopted dualistic strategies by the small and marginal cultivators on one side and by the wage-dependent cultivator households on the other. While the small and marginal farmers sold/or kept land fallow, the wage-dependent cultivators shifted to commercial cultivation to escape the crisis of acute shortage of female agricultural labour. The trends of consolidation are seen from consolidation of a huge area of wet land that was owned by a single family. In the entire history of the village, at no point of time was this type of ownership (concentration) of wet land seen.

The small and marginal farmers by 2009-10 survived in cultivation mostly substituting the female family labour for capital in paddy cultivation or some of them shifted to dry crops. Such cultivators were 11 per cent of households in the late 1970s. The per-household holding size fell to $1/4^{th}$ of the size obtained in 1999. Such major changes in land transfers transformed the social composition of land distribution across the social categories. The data suggests that although the area owned is small (1-2 and 2-5 acres), it is a large number of BC households that are dependent on land for livelihood.

The displacement of female labour from farming was associated with simultaneous displacement of them from traditional non-farm occupations which used to engage more female labour which provided additional financial support to agriculture. The new non-farm works that were accessible by the displaced farm households excluded female labour from the production role. Most of the occupations sprang up as a part of development were in the nature of "rent-seeking" and that did not have any role for female labour. Such development forced them to become housewives. The study has shown that the SCs and BCs that lent highest labour participation also reduced them into "housewives". This shift in demand for production labour is really a deterioration in the status of female labour.

The adoption of new strategies of substitution and cost saving also have changed the production roles of female labour. The role of female labour changed from hired labour to **female family farm labour** (unpaid labour), **feminized farm labour (by sliding down to low investment crops), pluri-activity female labour and female hired agricultural labour and additional farm activities that were previously done either by male labour or by machine.** These production roles show that female labour got marginalized. The state policies prioritized capital and feminized industrial employment and shifted agricultural labour by enrolling under MGNREGP to the corporate non-farm sector.

The case studies show that the land price bubble that was created by the land market resulted in speculative land business and consequently shift of crop land to non-farm business. The land distributed to weaker sections by the state in the early 1970s was dispossessed and the community services monetized. These changes in the rural political economy resulted in the occupational shifts of female labour and a significant number of them turned into family labour or housewives. The practice of keeping a difference in male and female agricultural wages has been carried to modern non-farm employment in industries. This model of development operates in favour of capital accumulation which left no space or necessary conditions created for female labour participation in development. These trends are further strengthened by a state policy intervention, taking women as objects and as a part of the strategy of the World Bank which in turn led to dispossession and displacement of the rural households from their livelihood assets. The Women's Self-Help Group policy through employment of women in micro enterprises as a part of strategy of the World Bank has ended in financial business along with the business of microfinance institutions in the liberalized financial market. This whole experiment proved to be counter-productive.

The state initiated the SHG programme with a stated objective of eradication of poverty and empowerment of women has been encouraged under a "new paradigm of development" that targets women's Self-Help Groups for (so-called) aid. This policy worked under the direction that SHG loan should strictly be used for asset creation. The creation of assets helps in enlarging the wage component in the overall value of production in the year. A close analysis of the empirical data shows that the world financial institutions with the nexus of the state, initiated the programme and expanded the business in finances for the accumulation of capital and shows that these non-state institutions are reducing the role of the state in the financial decision-making by acquiring monopoly over the financial market.

The state had become a spectator when the policies promulgated by it have been violated; while the state originally formulated the policy of the SHG loans for creating assets that support livelihoods, the monopoly finance made the state to include consumption borrowings in SHG loans subverting the asset building goal. The data shows that more than 75 per cent of the sample borrowers diverted their loan amount from asset creation to consumption, only the remaining 25 per cent borrowers who were already in some business or the other. This led neither to new employment nor asset creation. This unfolds the fact that the financial institutions did not desire the poor asset building. For expansion of financial business the loans for consumption have been included in the policy. This increased the share of profits and decreased the share of wages. These institutions so designed that SHGs got entangled in the model as the gap between profits and wages increase the rate of profits led to a further spurt in accumulation and spatial spread of the net of capital. For instance, the total amount sanctioned for grounding an income earning scheme has always been less than required and this amount has gone down in the IKP project. While the policy envisages that the enterprise yield an additional income but addition to what is not clear. The policy norm is to mobilize the savings of the SHG members to form this ratio of one-fourth of the bank loan but the financial institutions subverted this norm by resorting to mobilization of savings to a ratio of four times to that of bank loans by insisting that as a condition.

The study on SGSY shows that their funds were shifted in the name of community investment funds to the IKP project. These funds were meant earlier for allotment of the subsidy component to weaker sections. The non-state financial institutions negotiate with the state to shift these funds to invest in the infrastructure, training and skills for the SHG programme. These institutions also demanded a change in the rojgar programme that is structured for a cluster of rojgaries to individual and demanded to limit the role of the state to that of facilitator. These experiences indicate that the financial business had already expanded to dictating its terms to the state.

The micro-enterprises working with the SGSY government subsidy-cum-bank loan by the weaker sections are found weak both financially and organizationally. The subsidy amount fixed is so low and it also sealed the borrowings from the bank to the extent of subsidy. There is also reluctance on the part of borrowers in expansion of their business on account of limited market for their products. The banks also chose to support only those enterprises to lend that have been active for more than 15 years. The study confirmed that the borrowers use the loan for contingent expenditures of households. This neither generated new employment nor new investments for the weaker sections.

The study shows these vulnerable informal micro-enterprises are built on the support of social institutions, guilds like SHGs that have organizations of collective economic interests and use the social capital of community life. For instance, the micro-enterprises operate in a way where the husband purchases raw materials for the wife's enterprise, repairs the machines in the enterprise, parents pass on traditional skills and they are all using the house premises for setting up the enterprise. Such services are not accounted for market value and flow towards capital accumulation.

The Pavala Vaddi programme that has been initiated by the state of AP to substitute the subsidy programmes under IKP in the village show hardly any substantial increase in investment in micro enterprises out of the loans borrowed nor any generation of new employment. These enterprises also yield very low income. An integrated SHG programme called "The Livelihood Mission" advocated for spread of SHGs into the interior rural areas to eradicate poverty. This only helped in expansion of business in finances that would only yield profits for capital accumulation. On the development of the positive side of the SHG policy is that it has developed into a strong social network and contributed in containing the domestic violence. However this social development was an unintended gain.

The study has also taken up for examining the process and impact of industrialization on agrarian economy, on female labour as this area did undergo a rapid transition. This is done mainly to see how the development paradigm made a difference to the lives of the rural female labour force.

A case study of an industry (on BPL) done earlier yielded some evidence of new opportunities to young educated female labour. This industry was closed midway. For continuation of the study and comparison in temporal changes the industry like Pennar has been taken up. It presents certain trends that the female labour that availed of new industrial employment opportunities have been segregated into informal divisions as in BPL but worse conditions for the majority of workers and created more levels and ranks in the production process over the previous industry. This is because of choices of technology, allegedly created over supply of labour.

A well-performing formal industry engaged in manufacturing metallurgy for import substitution employed 2000 industry-specific skilled workers along with 600 casual labour (in 2009-10) indicating a new process of casualization of labour. The restructuring of industry into the liberalized and globalized market hit this labour hard by forcing them to opt for the voluntary retirement scheme. This type of retrenchment of the permanent skilled labour and industry-specific skills cannot be absorbed in other production industries. This process effects the female labour by creating separate segregated divisions that works under informal working conditions and at the lower end of production processes on intermittent tasks. Such segregated divisions are created for the sake of cost cutting on their wages which are adopted not only through casual, flexible, feminized informal and multitasking labour conditions but even on social security provisions. The cost cutting is also applied for not to include provisions for skill upgradation of this female labour. It is significant to note that instead of skill upgradation the industry introduced new devices that intensify their production.

The emergence of the labour contractor armed with the special Contract Labour Act worsened the exploitation of this labour as it ensures supply of required labour without any encumbrances to the industry. The industry uses social capital for recruitment. This has aggravated adverse conditions of labour over previous practice of advertising in daily newspapers. Industry preferring migrant labour and using social relations for recruitments accentuated the migration leading to housing problems to majority of the workers.

The study shows that the nature of capital accumulation is such that labour in general and female labour in particular are placed historically, at a great disadvantage in the changing economy of a rural village experiencing economic dynamism without overall forward moving development. This holds no promise for bettering of improving opportunities for female labour nor new avenues for their participation in a transitional economy.

Annexure for Chapters 1 to 4

Annexure 1: DIVISION OF FARMERS

Marginal farmers	0-2.5 acres
Small farmers	2.6-5.0 acres
Semi medium farmers	5.1-10 acres
Medium farmers	10.1-25 acres
Large farmers	25 and above acres.

Sample Survey Fourth Round April-September1952 has categorized the cultivators. 1. Tillers are those who cultivate their own land mainly with hired labour 2. Cultivators are defined as those who cultivate their own or sharecropping land with the help of other hh and partly with hired labour. 3. Share-croppers who take up cultivation of others land on crop sharing basis without hired labour. 4. Farmers are upper class cultivators. The study refers mainly to 2&3 categories.

Annexure 2:
Total Irrigated Land in the Village during 1984-85

Sl.No.	*Name of tank*	*Extent of land in acres*	*Percent*
1	Enki cheruvu	152.12	7.6
2	Pochamma cheruvu	43.24	2.2
3	Lella kunta	4.00	0.2
4	Bathula kunta	27.25	1.4
5	Kabil kastu (wet land for cultivation)	1671.35	94.5
6	Nadimila vagu	75.11	3.8
7	Kalinak (rain water)	13.31	0.7
8	Government land	13.08	0.7
9	Rasta (batalu)	6.38	0.3
10	Total	1991.03	100.0

Collected from Gram Panchayat office in 2009-10

Annexure 3: Female Occupational Particulars on Farm and Non-farm (Sample hh in no)

	1979					1989					1999				
Type of Occupation	*SC*	*BC*	*FC*	*Total*	*%*	*SC*	*BC*	*FC*	*Total*	*%*	*SC*	*BC*	*FC*	*Total*	*%*
Agriculture on own	9*	41*	34*	84	19.6	0	10	22	32	7.6	1	7	4	12	5.3
Agri-hired labour	56	125	16	197	46.0	59	129	12	200	47.3	15	31	2	48	21.2
Agri labour	0	0	0	0	0.0	1	0	0	1	0.2	0	0	0	0	0.0
Cane work	0	5	0	5	1.2	0	2	0	2	0.5	0	5	0	5	2.2
Potter	0	1	0	1	0.2	0	1	0	1	0.2	0	1	0	1	0.4
Wool spinning	0	1	0	1	0.2	0	0	0	0	0.0	0	0	0	0	0.0
Quarry	0	6	0	6	1.4	0	2	0	2	0.5	0	1	0	1	0.4
Construction	0	0	0	0	0.0	3	2	0	5	1.2	0	0	0	0	0.0
Dhobi	0	7	0	7	1.6	0	2	0	2	0.5	0	0	0	0	0.0
Midwife	1	0	1	2	0.5	0	0	0	0	0.0	0	0	0	0	0.0
Business	5	5	11	21	4.9	14	0	24	38	9.0	2	6	4	12	5.3
HH tailoring	0	3	0	3	0.7	0	0	7	7	1.7	0	4	6	10	4.4
Dairy	0	0	0	0	0.0	0	0	0	0	0.0	0	10	15	25	11.1
Government service	0	2	0	2	0.5	0	1	0	1	0.2	1	0	0	1	0.4
Industry	0	1	0	1	0.2	1	0	0	1	0.2	8	4	0	12	5.3
Mat weaving	0	0	0	0	0.0	0	4	0	4	0.9	0	0	0	0	0.0
Unemployed	0	0	0	0	0.0	0	0	0	0	0.0	3	6	12	21	9.3
Housewives	3	63	32	98	22.9	14	63	50	127	30.0	4	2	72	78	34.5
Total	74	260	94	428	100.0	92	216	115	423	100.0	34	77	115	226	100.0

Vanamala ICSSR Report 2003.

Annexure 4: Family Labour and Hired Labour– Joint and Nuclear Family in 1979

	Forward Castes				*Backward Castes*				*Scheduled Castes*			
	Family. Agri. Labour		*Hired Agri. Labour*		*Family Agri. Labour*		*Hired Agri. Labour*		*Family. Agri. Labour*		*Hired Agri. Labour*	
	Actual	*%*	*Actual*	*%*	*Actual*	*%*	*Actual*	*%*	*Actual*	*%*	*Actual*	*%*
Joint Family	24	71	10	29	34	32	75	68	6	15	34	84
Nuclear Family	12	82	4	18	7	12	50	88	3	12	26	88
	36		14		41		125		9		56	

Source: Vanamala, *Mainstream*, March 13, 1982.

Annexure 5: The Livestock Possessed by the Sample Households in 1995-96 (livestock in nos.)

Type of animal	*SC*	*BCs*	*FCs*	*Total*
She buffaloes	0	12	8	20
Bullocks	0	7	2	9
Cows	0	2	0	2
Goat and sheep	0	120	0	120
Total	0	141	10	151

Source: Vanamala ICSSR Report (2003).

Annexure 6: Livestock Possessed by the Sample Households in 2009-10

Caste	*Bullocks*	*Buffaloes*	*Sheep*
SC	0	0	0
BC	0	5	80
FC	2	1	0
Total	2	6	2

Collected from respondents

Annexure 7: Multi Occupational Combination

Combinations of Occupations	*Average income per month in Rs.*	*Work available for months in a year in number*	*Income from agricultural sector in Rs.*	*Total income from non-farm per annum in Rs.*
Stiching+	650	4	–	(1x2) 2600
agricultural labour	–		3000	
Bangle business+	1500	4	–	6000
Stiching	650	6		3900
+cultivation		4	8000	2600
Diary+	2000	12	6000	24000
Grazing+	6000	Consolidated per annum		
Cane work	800	8		6400
Agricultural labour+Broom stick making	100	3	3000	300
Agricultural labour+Leaf plate making	1500		3000	1500
Agricultural labour+Cane work	800	3	3000	800 2400
Dairy+ Agricultural labour	2000	12	3000	24000
Cultivation+pot business	100	3	4000	300

Source: Vanamala ICSSR Report (2003).

Focused Group Discussion Method: This is another method used for the work to capture data from various age, social, occupational and class backgrounds across generations. They cannot give wrong information as there are other women in the gathering. There are several issues that affect women's daily lives. But the cultural norms in the society do not permit them to share it in the public discussions. But general narrations they do about others keeping some cases in mind in the village are important. The issues like intra-household relations and relations between wife and husband, dowry payments and dowry deaths, issues on alcohol consumption, issues on community life and clashes over property and political issues like opinion on participation of women in the Gram Sabha and other issues that bother women including issues related to power centres[19] can be freely gathered in focused group discussion.

Focused Group Discussion

The women gathered for focused group discussion have given an account of traditions and cultural forms of identity of women in the former rural agrarian society. An interesting and significant practice in the villages was to keep girls' share (for each girl in the family, in kind) from total paddy produce before it was used for home consumption. The value of this yield was saved in the girl's account. This was meant for her social security. (Inspired by this practice, Madhu Kishwar, an activist, made a TV programme). This practice has been reversed and replaced by the dowry payment to the bridegroom's family in the modern economy.

The second aspect they discussed was about the cultural practice called 'ILLITAM' (adoption) that was in wide practice in the society prior to 80s. The families that did not have a son (patrileaneal lineage) to own the landed property, the daughter could be the legal hire legitimately. The marriage contract in such a case involves the bridegroom moving to the girl's residence instead of the girl moving to her husband's house (as in patrileaneal tradition). This practice disappeared after the late 1980s, leaving no scope for girls to own land.

On arack consumption the women stated that it is consumed by all the social groups almost every day except Brahmin and Vaishya castes. They stated that women also consume arack but on rare occasions like- visits of the guests, specific religious celebrations and on occasions of deaths and births. The arack for the female farm labour has become a part of wage payments. The respondents stated that the friction among the household members was common after arack consumption. The arack market made its way into agriculture. The female labour who earned paddy as wages in kind have moved to arack as wages for their consumption.

The respondents expressed unanimously that the present generation is relatively free from controls and other torture on daughters-in-law that were widely in practice in previous generations. The family food serving and eating habits have changed towards providing freedom to women.

Some women observed that ever since women joined the Self-Help Groups' (SHG) men are cautious to scold or beat them. They stated that women gained confidence with the social power of SHG. Some women have stated that the present generation women are educated, earning and are well-informed about their rights and expressed that 'younger women have become relatively autonomous and question any unwarranted deed on them'.

It is interesting as observed by the group that there is a social restriction on free mobility of young girls in the public place, which is also honoured by them to oblige the elders in the family. They also expressed that because of such practices women hesitate to participate in public activities like contesting for the elections for public representation, participation in Gram Sabha meetings and to discharge the duties as women sarpanches.

The observations on dowry payments show that no woman in the group got married without paying dowry. The discussion reveals that as time is advancing, the amount of dowry offered has been increasing. For instance, this is clear from the case of a family that has received dowry to four sons over a period. The first son was offered Rs 30,000 twelve years ago. The second was offered 1.20 lakhs ten years back, the third was offered 2.60 lakhs eight years back. The last son was offered 3.50 lakhs five years back. Thus the dowry has been increasing in a linear upward direction. It is also observed that this increase is not based on the achievements of the groom like his educational achievements or owning of property. It is entirely due to socio-economic changes in the region. This is an indication of increasing monetization of social relations.

It is very striking that both the husband and wife are educated up to the seventh class. The husband works as a casual worker in a precarious job while the wife remains a housewife. However one can argue that the educational achievements have helped women to rescue themselves from the victimization of bad customs like female foeticides, etc. These women are keen to work in industries partly to meet the new obligations of the increased demand of private English medium education to their children and the social dignity associated with it in the new society. (It is very important to note that the "housewifizaton" or to get confined to domestic work, when incomes increase was social dignity in the agrarian rural social system in 1979. This has changed for young women and they want to work for social dignity). This change in social value is tapped by new industries. The following examples of female labour elabourated it.

The new aspirations and consequent compulsions to work in industries became the base for fixing low wages for women in the new industries. The garment export industry has fixed a target to stitch 500 pieces per day which takes more than 12 hours. The wages are awfully low and they suffer pain in the neck and waist with that oppressive work. The families of these women think that the opportunity cost of this work is very low. Therefore they prefer their spouse to be at home catering to domestic chores of the family, tutoring children, caring for elders, etc.

The changes in sharing the household expenditure by husband and wife have been narrated by the women of the present generation. It is of two kinds. In one type the husband shares a fixed amount from his earnings in the case of the earning wife. The rest of the expenditure he expects the wife to bear. The major additional new expenditure of the household is for children's education that has been progressively increasing along with new social demands that need cash. The women noted that children's education expenditure has been ever increasing. So also the cash demand has gone up for carrying gifts to birthday celebrations and picnics. Women work for longer hours to meet these needs. The husband never feels the need to curtail his economic freedom while women do curtail their freedom by taking up additional work to meet the additional needs.

The second trend in the case of a non-earning wife the entire expenditure is met by the husband. However in this case also the restriction of freedom of spending is observed. The husband purchases the entire goods for the family on the pretext that the goods are purchased from wholesale shops located outside the village. In this case women's freedom in choice of goods is affected.

Women hardly spend on their health (There are many cases of misscarriages even among the age group of 20-30 years). The health does not take a place in the budget and expenditure of the household. These practices are related to limited work opportunities for women. The work available is opened in segmented, low wage and unskilled market that perpetuates gender inequality. For instance, the policy SHG proposes self-employment in microenterprises at the household level. These choices of work yield low returns to women with heard work and long time.

The current domestic division of the household labour is a response to the gendered labour market in which women are paid lower wages for their work than men. This type of inequality keeps women in low aspiration over development of their capabilities through training. This in turn sets the level of social expectations of the domestic division of labour.

Annexure Chapter 6

Annexure 1

Expansion of Private/for Profit Micro Finance Institutions (MFI): *Forbes* magazine[1] listed seven microfinance institutes of India that can compete with the top 50 microfinance institutions of the world. They are ranked like–Bandhan and Microcredit Foundation of India that ranked 13th. Saadhana Microfin Society ranked 15th, Saadhana Microfin Society and Grameen Koota ranked 19th place. The Sharada Women's Association for Weaker Sections ranked 23rd, SKS Microfinance Private Ltd ranked 44th and Asmitha Microfin Ltd is placed in the 29th[2] rank. The author observed that most of these institutions have converted themselves from Non-Government Organizations (NGO). The NGOs which were registered under "public purpose" and started through donor and philanthropic funds as non-profit Credit Societies with a focus on poverty and other forms of interventions that could benefit the poor, have moved from "not-for-profit" to "for-profit" status (Reddy, 2011)[3] by obtaining the status of Non-Banking Financial Company (NBFC). NBFC is a company registered under the Companies Act, 1956 of India, engaged in the business of loans and advances, acquisition of shares, stocks, bond share-purchase, insurance business, or chit business. It is also important to note that this process is in fast progress in the country. An increasing number of microfinance institutions (MFIs) are seeking non-banking finance company (NBFC) status from RBI to get wide access to funding, including bank finance. This is happening at a time when banks are seeking to increase their exposure to microcredit. In addition, MFIs and NGOs are looking at broad-basing their sources of funds. These include raising funds through equity investments, debt funds, external commercial borrowings (ECBs), venture capital funds, grants and contributions. An NGO and an MFI could operate in the form of a trust by registering under the Commissioner of Trusts and Charity or a company Section 25 with the Registrar of Companies or else an NBFC under RBI norms.

Annexure 2

Working of Private MFIs: A review of MFI conducted jointly by the Reserve Bank of India and a few major banks have made the following observations:

- Some of the microfinance institutions (MFIs) financed by banks or acting as their intermediaries or partners appear to be focusing on relatively better banked areas, including areas covered by the SHG-Bank linkage programme. Competing MFIs were operating in the same area, and trying to reach out to the same set of poor, resulting in multiple lending and overburdening of rural households.
- Many MFIs supported by banks were not engaging themselves in capacity building and empowerment of the groups to the desired extent. The MFIs were disbursing loans to the newly formed groups within 10–15 days of their formation, in contrast to the practice. The IKP SHG–Bank linkage programme, takes about six to seven months for group formation and nurturing. As a result, cohesiveness and a sense of purpose were not being built up in the groups formed by these MFIs.
- Banks, as principal financiers of MFIs, do not appear to be engaging them with regard to their systems, practices and lending policies with a view to ensuring better transparency and adherence to best practices. In many cases, no review of MFI operations was undertaken after sanctioning the credit facility.

Following the crisis in Andhra Pradesh wherein the state government had asked local MFIs to close down operations as they competed with the state lending programme called Velugu. It is observed that the banks are becoming increasingly sceptical to lend to non-NBFC MFIs.

Annexure 2: District-wise Disbursements Made Under Self-Help Group-Bank Linkage Programme in Andhra Pradesh (1999-00 to 2001-02) (Rs in Lakhs)

Districts	*1999-00*	*RANK*	*2000-01*	*RANK*	*2001-02*	*RANK*
Srikakulam	128.199	13	1032.287	2	2153.716	2
East Godavari	1017.535	1	2094.06	1	3409.055	1
West Godavari	123.476	15	410.154	16	899.752	16
Guntur	33.787	20	505.246	14	1335.178	6
Vizianagaram	20.596	21	182.447	21	473.351	21
Vishakapatnam	232.44	10	754.689	7	1434.196	5
Medak	472.476	3	690.682	9	866.191	17
Mahbubnagar	420.915	5	1026.126	3	1613.875	4
Warangal	300.204	8	881.613	5	1824.695	3
Ranga Reddy	636.317	2	604.428	10	862.272	18
Nalgonda	215.94	11	407.389	17	1207.871	10
Nizamabad	79.651	16	419.878	15	917.587	14
Khammam	124.979	14	573.992	11	1209.572	8
Karimnagar	336.845	6	926.826	4	735.231	20
Adilabad	64.94	17	334.007	19	1036.79	12
Prakasam	63.313	18	529.703	13	1138.239	11
Nellore	306.755	7	552.212	12	960.959	13
Kurnool	143.04	12	401.606	18	847.238	19
Anantapur	63.266	19	321.391	20	913.468	15
Cuddapah	0.73	22	158.315	22	387.497	22
Krishna	274.475	9	867.261	6	1208.405	9
Chittoor	429.387	4	738.123	8	1274.046	7
Total	**5489.267**		**14312.434**		**26709.188**	

Source: Rajya Sabha Unstarred Question No. 2034, dated March 11, 2003.

Exemptions Grsanted to NBFCs Engaged in Microfinance Activities

The Task Force on Supportive Policy and Regulatory Framework for Microfinance set up by NABARD in 1999 provided various recommendations. Accordingly, it was

Number of SHG Members in Andhra Pradesh

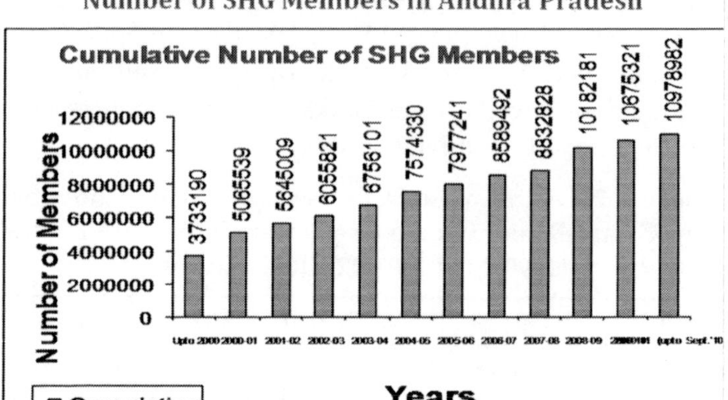

Figure: Illustrative SHG Federation

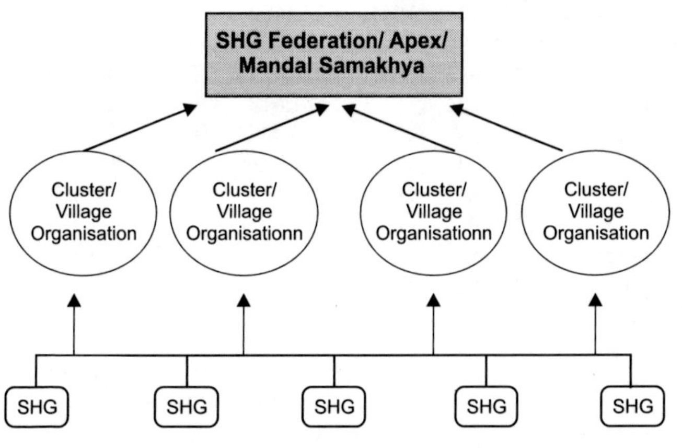

Source: Reddy, C.S. and S. Manak, 2005

decided to exempt NBFCs which are engaged in micro financing activities, licensed under Section 25 of the Companies Act, 1956, and which do not accept public deposits, from the purview of Sections 45-IA (registration), 45-IB (maintenance of liquid assets) and 45-IC (transfer of profits to the Reserve Fund) of the RBI Act, 1934.

Schemes in IKP

The important schemes implemented by the Rural

Development Department at the district level through DRDA include:

1. Indira Kranti Patham (IKP)
2. Swarnajayanti Gram Swarojgar Yojana (SGSY)
3. Revolving Fund
4. Pavala Vaddi
5. Gruhuni
6. Old Age Pensions (OAP)

ANNEXURES FOR CHAPTER VII

Annexure 1. Wage and social security benefits to the workers under import substitution era.

Table 1 shows the number of male and female workers working in one shift of the Pennar industry. The same number of workers work in the other two shifts.

Table 1. Employment Structure of the Permanent Workers (in one shift)

Cold roll department	*Permanent*	*Junior staff*	*Contract*
Male	100	100	80
Female	Nil	Nil	Nil

The qualifications of all these workers at the time of recruitment was only 10th class. The wages and social security benefits of these workers are as follows.

Table 2. Wage Structure of the Permanent Male Skilled Operators (Case of Raju)(in Rs)

Basic in 2009	*DA*	*HRA*	*Gross*	*When Casual*	*Service*	*PF deductions*	*Subsidized food PM*	*Free transp*
6500	4000	1200	15000	600	18 years	1300	200	-

Table (2) shows the pay slip of the workers that contains the details of basic and other social security provisions. Over and above these wages the workers are eligible for **Family Insurance** up to Rs one lakh. The expenditure incurred over and above this amount on treatment the industry shared in several cases. The industry has appointed an **on-the-campus-**

doctor and a compounder. The industry distributed bonus to workers around Rs 12,000 every year. The Nagarjuna Steels had given house sites and Pennar sanctioned PF for construction of houses on those plots to permanent workers. These workers enjoy subsidized food, free tea and transport provided by the industry.

NOTES

1. The previous and present patwary, sarpanch, Machkuri were interviewed covering three generations.
2. Htt//en.wikipedia.org/wiki/filowiki_letter_w.svg February 2009. 34 The MFI cannot have access to public deposits and cannot lend more than Rs 50,000 to a single borrower/group of borrowers. Mathew Titus, Sadhan's executive director, said, "Banks find it difficult to lend to MFIs in the absence of sufficient collateral. Hence, they ask MFIs to widen their capital base, which is possible only by transforming themselves into NBFCs." The central bank tightened the noose on banks lending to NBFCs in its latest set of guidelines but industry sources feel that this is unlikely to have an impact on banks funding NBFCs functioning as MFIs. According to the recent guidelines, the exposure of a bank to a single NBFC cannot exceed 10% of the bank's capital funds as per its last audited balance sheet.
3. Transformation" from "Not for Profit" to "For Profit". Almost all "not for profit" credit societies started through donor and philanthropic funds which were grants with focus on poverty and interventions that could benefit the poor. Registered under "public purpose" with donor money for "larger social good". No "residual claims" either on current income (no dividends) or on liquidation proceeds. Whatever residue goes either to a society/trust of similar nature or to the state. How to move from "not for profit" (charitable) to "for profit" (commercial) NBFC's Minimum Capital Requirement is Rs 2 crore. The transfer of the "society" capital to NBFC is by creating Mutual Benefit Trusts (MBTs) which can invest for profit. By making the members of credit societies as members of MBTs and lend or donate or grant society funds to these members to invest in MBTs. With MBT money by floating NBFC (Narasimha Reddy, power points presented to CDS and ICSSR Seminar 2011).

References

Agarwal, Bina (1998), Disinherited Peasants-Disadvantaged Workers: A Gender Perspective on Land and Livelihood *Economic & Political Weekly,* Vol. 33, No. 13, March 26-April 26.

Agarwal, Bina, A Gendered Agrarian Transition, *Journal of Agrarian Change,* Vol. 3, No. 172, January-April 2003.

Alpa and Barbara Harris White (2011), Resurrecting Scholarship on Agrarian Transformation, *Economic & Political Weekly,* Vol. XI, No. 39.

Annual Report (2009-10) Pennar makes it possible, Pennar Industries Ltd.

Ashok Kumar, Methukuseema charitra-samscruithy Manzeera Rachithala Sangham (2008).

Bateman, Milford (2003), 'Why Can't Microfinance Work'?, Cambridge University Press.

Bateman, Milford (2010), 'Why Doesn't' Microfinance work?' *The Destructive Rise of Local Neo-liberalism*, Zed Books, London, New York.

Bhaduri, Amit (2006), *Employment and Development: Essays from an Unorthodox Perspective*, Oxford University Press.

Bhalla, G.S. (2007), 49th Conference, The Indian Society of Labour Economics, Hyderabad.

Department of Rural Development (2009), Repot on Credit Related Issues Under SGSY Government of India.

Dhanagare (1987), Green Revolution and Social Inequalities, *Economic & Political Weekly,* Vol. 22, No. 19/21 May Annual Number.

Government of India, Ministry of Finance (2007) Report on Expert Group on Agricultural Indebtedness.

Habib Haroon Editorial, *The Hindu* Daily, April 5, 2011.

Hand Book of Statistics (*2004-05*), Chief Planning Officer, Medak District.

Hand Book of Statistics (2005-06), Chief Planning Officer, Medak District.

Hand Book of Statistics (2006-07) Chief Planning Officer, Medak District.

Hand Book of Statistics (2007-08), Chief Planning Officer, Medak District.

Harris Barbara (1997), Green Revolution to Rural Industrialization, *Economic & Political Weekly*, June 2.

Harvey, David (2005), *The New Imperialism*, Oxford University Press.

Hindu Editorial, November 14, 2011.

http://www.ngosindia.com/resources/ngo_registration1.php/CAF India

Hudis, Peter and Anderson, Kevin B. (eds.) (2005), The Luxemburg Rosa Reader, Cornerstone Publications, Kharagpur.

ICFTU (2004), A Trade Union Guide to Globalisation, 2nd edition, International Confederation of Free Trade Unions, Brussels. ILO.

Kamalakar, K.G. (ed), (2008), *Micro Finance in India*, Sage Publishers, New Delhi.

Kelkar, Govind, Gender and Productive Assets: Implications for Women's Economic Security and Productivity, *Economic & Political Weekly*, June 4, 2011.

Kumar, Ashok, Methukuseema charitra-samscruithy Manzeera Rachithala Sangham (2008).

Land Committee Recommendations (2006), Submitted to Government of Andhra Pradesh.

Lemire, Beverly (ed), (2001) *Women and Credit: Women Credit and the Creation of Opportunity: A Historical Overview*, Oxford, New York.

Levien, Michael (2011), *Special Economic Zones and Accumulation by Dispossession in India*, Blackwell Publishers and also see *Journal of Agrarian Change*, Vol. 11, No. 4, October 2011, pp. 454-483.

Mark, Hormstrom (1984), *Industry and Inequality: The Social Anthropology of Indian Labour*, Cambridge University Press, Cambridge.

Marx, Karl, *Capital* 1 (1977), *A Critique of Political Economy*, Vol. 1 Translated from the Third German Edition by Samuel Moore and Edward Aveling and Edited by Frederick Engels, Progress Publisher. Mies, Maria and Veronika Bennholdt_Thomsen "The Subsistence Perspective", Saturday, January 20, 2007 at 12:24 pm PST. Also see Maria Mies "Colonization and housewifization" caring labour an archive http:/caring labour.wordpress. com2010.

Network (2009), *India Infrastructure Report: Land: A Critical Resource for Infrastructure*, Oxford University Press, New Delhi.

NSSO 2003-04.

Patancheru, Notified Municipal Industrial Areas Service Society (2008),

10th Anniversary Souvenir.

Patnaik, Prabhat and others (1998), "Crisis in Agriculture and Response" Raman Uddaraju Memorial Foundation & AP Rythu Sangham, Hyderabad.

Patnaik, Utsa (2008), *The Republic of Hunger and Other Essays,* Three Essays Collective, Amagaon.

Pearson, Ruth (2001), *Continuity and Change-Towards a Conclusion,* (ed) Beverly Lemire, Ruth Pearson and Gail Gampbell, Oxford University Press, New York.

Perselle, Praksh and Sanjeev (eds), (2004), *Investing in Social Capital: Comparative Perspectives on Civil Society, Participation and Governance*, Sage Publishers, New Delhi.

Posthuma, Anne and Nathan Dev (eds.) (2010), *Labour in Global Production Networks in India*, Oxford University Press.

Rajen, Vittal (1989), Small Voices, Small Victories, the Deccan Development Society, (2010), *Economic & Political Weekly,* Vol. XLV, No. 49, December 4.

Rao, Bhaskara (2009), National Network Enabling Self-Help Group Movement, NNE-Networks.

Rao, Bhaskara, Report on National Network Enabling Self-Help Movement (NN-ABLE) 2009, APMAS.

Razavi, Shahra (2003), Introduction: An Agrarian Change, Gender and Land Rights, *Journal of Agrarian Change*, Vol. 3, Nos. 1 & 2 January and April, pp. 2-32.

Reddy Y.V. (2009), "India's Financial Sector in Current Times", *Economic and Political Weekly*, 7th November.

Reddy, Bahaman (2010) Agricultural Crisis, *Veekshanam* (Telugu Monthly), August.

Reddy, C.S. and Sandeep Manak (2005), APMAS International Mahila Abhivruddhi Society.

Report Card on Special Economic Zones (2009) Intercultural Resources, New Delhi.

Report on Fifth Economic Census (2005), Medak District, Directorate of Economics and Statistics, Government of Andhra Pradesh, Hyderabad.

Report on the National Commission on Enterprises for the Unorganized Sector, Government of India (2007) known as Arjun Sen Gupta Committee.

Rodger, Gerry (2007), Decent Work, Social Inclusion and Development in *Indian Journal of Human Development,* Vol. 1, No. 12007.

Rodger, Gerry (2007), Labour Market Flexibility and Decent Work' in Ocampo, Jose Antonio and Jomo, K.S. (eds.), *Towards Full and*

Decent Employment, Orient Longman, Published in Association with the United Nations.

SANET_MG – on Poor Women Farmers Report of Rheagala, in Medak District (2006), Internet. Sundaresan (2011), International Conference on Applied Economics, "Special Economic Zone and Accumulation by Dispossession", Blackwell Publishers.

Santa, Barbara (2009), Revisiting Micro Credit/Microfinance as a Development Strategy for an Inclusive Growth: A Global Perspective, Orfalea Centre For Global & International Studies University if California.

Sanyal, Kalyan, *Rethinking Capitalist Development: Primitive Accumulation, Governmentality and Post-Colonialism*, Routledge, Taylor & Francis Group, London, New York, New Delhi, 2007.

Satish, P.V. and Pimbert (1999), Reclaiming Diversity, Restoring Livelihoods in Medak District: A Study by Dekkan Development Centre, Internet.

Sen Gupta, Arjun (2010), Towards a Campaign for Right to Employment, *IJLE*, Vol. 53, No. 1, 2010.

Sriram, M.S. (2010a), "Commercialization of Micro Finance in India: A Discussion of the Emperor's Apparel", *Economic and Political Weekly*, 12th June.

Vaidyanathan (2010), *Agricultural Growth in India: Role of Technology, Incentives and Institutions*, Oxford University Press.

Vanamala (1981), Women Labour in Telangana Village, *Mainstream*, August 1.

—— (1982), Hired and Family Labour Among Women, *Mainstream*, March 13.

—— (2001), Structural Adjustment, Flexible Employment Labour Markets and Female Labour: A Study on India and South East Asian Countries, Indian Secretariat, ICSSR and Dutch Secretariat WOTRO.

—— (2001), Informalization and Feminization of a Formal Sector Industry—A Case Study, *Economic & Political Weekly*, XXXVI, No. 26, June 30.

—— (2001), Impact of Industrialization on Female Employment, ICSSR Report mimeo.

—— (2010b)"Micro Finance a Fairy Tale Turns into a Nightmare", *Economic and Political Weekly*, 23, October.

—— (2003), Impact of Industrialization on Female Employment, Report Submitted to ICSSR (Unpublished).

White, Barbara Harris (2003), *Working India: Essays on Society and Economy*, Cambridge University Press.